The 112 Meditations from the Book of Divine Wisdom

The 112 Meditations from the Book of Divine Wisdom

The meditations from the
Vijnana Bhairava Tantra,
with commentary and guided practice

Lee Lyon

The 112 Meditations
from the Book of Divine Wisdom:
The meditations from the *Vijnana Bhairava Tantra*,
with commentary and guided practice

Author: Lee Lyon

ISBN: 978-0-578-60465-7

E-Book ISBN: 978-0-578-60467-1

Library of Congress Control Number: 2019918455

© 2019 Foundation for Integrative Meditation

Website: integrativemeditation.org

Book and cover design: kenessondesign.com
Cover Image: Stone Shiva at Badami Caves, India
© Radiokafka/Adobe Stock
Photograph of author: Nancy Dahl

Contents

Contents

To all those seeking to know their true Self.

Foreword

The ancient meditation practices compiled in the *Vijnana Bhairava* have been elucidated by sages for centuries. It is one of the most highly regarded texts in Kashmir Shaivism, a non-dual Tantra tradition which emerged in Kashmir, India, twelve hundred years ago. Prior to it being codified in writing sometime around the eighth century, many of the methods of the *Vijnana Bhairava* were passed down orally for thousands of years. Its wisdom is eternal as is its source—your true nature as unbounded Consciousness, free beyond anything the ordinary mind can imagine.

Our typical experience of consciousness is the limited awareness of our mind. When we are awake, we are conscious of the world through our senses and we're conscious of our inner world of thoughts, feeling, intuitions, sensations, etc. What the ancient yogis discovered while exploring the nature of consciousness through meditation was that consciousness doesn't have to be limited by the ordinary sense of body and mind. They discovered that there's a universal Consciousness, an unbounded Consciousness that experiences the entire realm of creation as its own Self in the same way that our limited consciousness experiences our mind and body as itself. This profound understanding permeates the sublime teachings of Kashmir Shaivism. By convention, capitalized "Consciousness" refers to that universal Consciousness while small "c" "consciousness" refers to our ordinary mind. In the same way

"Self" refers to that universal Consciousness and "self" refers to our ordinary sense of being the mind and body. The Tantra tradition points out that the essential nature of Consciousness is woven into every thread of reality. In fact, it is the very warp and woof of all that is.

Modern physics since Einstein has pointed out that all matter is energy. The ancient sages refined their consciousness through focused meditation practices until they could directly know that energy, which they called Shakti—the power of universal Consciousness to create all forms. Like Einstein, they saw that all forms are a dance of vibrating energy. The ancient yogis came to know that the energy of the universe has as its basic quality Consciousness. It was the late Sir David Bohm, the brilliant protégé of Einstein, who added to Einstein's discovery that all matter is energy, the insight that the energy making up all matter, all that is known and experienced, has the quality of consciousness. In this way there's a striking similarity between the ancient wisdom of the sages and modern quantum physics.

The *Vijnana Bhairava* is a collection of 112 focusing techniques called *dharanas*. Meditation masters have used these for thousands of years to directly know the nature of Consciousness as all-inclusive unity awareness. These techniques can now be seen as ancient mind/brain hacks for taking individual consciousness beyond the confines of everyday waking state experience into the expansive transcendent states that have traditionally been the purview of spiritual and religious disciplines. Transcendent states are now being scientifically studied in the lab. We can see that a variety of yogic and Buddhist practices have profound impacts on the mind/brain. The changes that can be seen in various brain imaging studies show that these ancient practices change not only our thoughts and ways of experiencing ourselves and others, they actually physically alter the brain. They even change neuronal circuitry. The experimental subjects in these studies used just their conscious attention to focus in particular ways, be it on the breath, emptiness, loving kindness, or compassion. With repeated meditative focusing, their brains and their experiences of everyday life changed. These types of focusing techniques are exactly what Lee Lyon's guided practices from the ancient *Vijnana Bhairava* provide the reader.

Lee Lyon has been studying, practicing and teaching the timeless wisdom of the *Vijnana Bhairava* for over forty years. For the last decade he has endeavored to translate the original Sanskrit text of the *dharanas* in a way that would free it from the cultural sediment that encumbers it. The intent of Lyon's translation is to make it accessible to all those who want to benefit from the powerful methods for directly experiencing the expansive field of awareness that we call Consciousness. He has honed these translations through working with students in year-long courses, workshops and meditation programs. Like the oral tradition that first gave rise to this compilation of meditation practices, Lyon has worked with western students to insure that the language serves the true intent of the *Vijnana Bhairava* to open your innate Consciousness to knowing your Self-luminous nature.

Over millennia sages and saints taught practical means for leaving behind the confines of the ordinary mind to enter the realm of universal Consciousness, pure non-dual unity awareness. Knowing this for oneself is the true goal of all yogas, all non-dual paths; it is the heart essence of true meditation. Teachers and practitioners from many traditions will find Lyon's translation provides the practices that empower people to directly experience the sublime state of boundless, all-embracing Consciousness, free from concepts—religious or spiritual.

—**Lawrence Edwards,** PhD, LMHC, BCN Senior Fellow,
Faculty member, New York Medical College
Founder and director,
the Anam Cara Meditation Foundation
Author, *Awakening Kundalini: The Path to Radical Freedom,*
The Soul's Journey: Guidance from the Divine Within, and *Kali's Bazaar*

Introduction

The *Vijnana Bhairava* is a compendium of 112 ecstatic meditations from the 8th century Shaivite tradition in Kashmir. Acknowledged as one of the supreme jewels of the Tantric tradition of northern India, this much loved text had remained largely obscure until its rediscovery last century. The sublime view of reality presented in this text is infectious and compelling. One of the great hallmarks of this tradition is its unabashed and enthusiastic engagement of all aspects of our life experience, even the unspiritual, as wonderful, natural gateways into our true nature.

I first came across this text forty years ago while studying and traveling in India with Swami Muktananda. It had just been translated into English by a gifted scholar of the Kashmiri Shaivite tradition. I was part of a team of meditation teachers at the time, and we were thrilled to have access to these practices. The meditations gave us a glimpse into an incredibly awakened and strikingly modern approach to spirituality that would evolve into the philosophy of Kashmir Shaivism in the centuries that followed.

Of all the different spiritual traditions that I have studied over the years, the meditations and the inherent feeling and attitude embodied in these practices are closest to my heart. For many years, as my fellow teachers and I traveled the world to lead meditation retreats, I always had a copy of the *Vijnana Bhairava* I tucked into my suitcase. While I rarely had time to read it, just seeing it I felt like I had an old friend with me.

Although couched in the beautiful metaphors of the time, the ideas and practices in this text are timeless in nature. Many of the meditations speak directly to our modern sensibilities and loves. The basic teaching is to penetrate through the surface appearance of our lives into the pure energy behind the form. It is through engaging the deeper energy in any experience, pleasurable or difficult, ecstatic or terrifying, that we move through the appearance of separation into the ever present Oneness.

The text is more than just a collection of extraordinary and powerful meditation instructions. It embodies an ecstatic and life affirming world view. Rather than conceptualizing spirituality, here it is approached more like music or art. We can feel the author's direct contact with life—intimate, kind, amused, amazed, delighted—always trying to get us to relate to our experience, to life, to consciousness, to actually engage it rather than just observe or be mindful of it.

It has been my privilege to teach these practices for over forty years now to both small and large groups of people. Even people who think themselves incapable of meditating find themselves easily entering new and altered states. Although traditionally considered a text for advanced meditators, many people with no formal experience in meditation have extraordinary shifts in consciousness using these practices.

Over the years many students would ask me where they could find these meditations. I would happily direct them to the original translation that I had studied for so many years, only to discover that they found the density of Sanskrit terms made it almost impossible for them to understand the text. It is for this reason that ten years ago I undertook translating the original verses into simple, clear and concise instructions that anyone could explore with ease.

The original Sanskrit reflects an extraordinary level of clarity, intelligence, poetic grace, delight and playfulness that is almost impossible to capture in English. Each verse here has been translated as literally as possible to help convey the actual meditation instruction embedded in the rich, multidimensional original. A short commentary and an example of how each meditation might be practiced, has been added after each verse to help explain the instruction.

These powerfully concentrated instructions known as *dharanas,* show us how to focus our attention on the many different aspects of our life experience in a such a way as to propel us beyond our thinking into the meditative state of unity—unity with our inner self and with all of life. Each of the original meditations is compressed into two simple rhythmic lines. The brevity of the instruction is intentional, giving a powerful and clear focus to our attention as well as aiding us in committing the meditations to memory.

The original text tells us that it offers 112 meditations, yet there are clearly 114 verses in this portion of the text. It is understood that certain meditations comprise two verses, although it is not clear which ones. As a bow to tradition, I have chosen to cite the number 112 in my title and, at the same time, to present all 114 verses as meditations.

The first instructions begin with subtle variations on classical yogic breathing techniques, honoring the more traditional approaches to meditation. However, soon the text starts to explore other dimensions of our consciousness, embracing practices that take us into the energy body, the thought-free state, the void, spaciousness, the world of our senses and the extraordinarily rich spectrum of our human emotions.

As the text progresses, contemplative practices are woven in, culminating in some of the world's most sublime meditations on Oneness. By repeatedly encouraging us to see the spontaneous unity behind the surface appearance of life, and to step into our true Self, the sublime and thought-free awareness that is our true center—the text holds its place as one of the crown jewels of human thought.

The message of this text is life affirming, dramatic and uncompromising. It suggests that by shifting our attention through subtle gestures of focus, we can enter the experience of unconditioned, utterly free consciousness, our true nature, sometimes in an instant. The text insists that this awareness is inherent in every human being and hovers just behind the surface of our normal attention. The experience is common to all who notice it in the background of their thinking, quietly waiting to be included.

There are many different types of meditation in the text, recognizing always the incredible richness and uniqueness of our individual consciousness. Each of us will be naturally drawn to those meditations that engage us. Some people will prefer the more classical breathing and energy flow meditations near the beginning of the book, while others will find it easier to begin with some of the more contemplative or life engaging meditations later in the book.

It is not necessary to read the text in sequence. When you find a meditation that you are drawn to, it can be of great value to repeat it on a regular basis for a while, allowing the experience of it to stabilize and deepen.

Although written over a thousand years ago, the meditations have a universal quality. They seem to arise from a timeless dimension of our collective humanity. They are as effective in returning us to our true nature today as they were centuries ago when they were first written.

May you, like so many others, be inspired by the meditations that follow.

A mighty flame follows a tiny spark.

—Dante

The
Meditations

1.
The beginning points of the breath

Breathing in—down. Breathing out—up. The One whose nature it is to create is this flow. Fix the mind on the two places where each breath begins and enter the state of divine fullness.

—Verse 24

When we breathe in, a subtle energy flows down the middle of our body. When we breathe out, the energy rises up. Just before each inbreath and outbreath, there is a timeless moment when the breath is suspended in pure energy. In this moment you touch the utterly free and spontaneous energy that creates all things: the universal life force itself. By focusing on these two places where the breath originates, our awareness gradually begins to steady in our true Self, the state of divine fullness.

The physical location of the two beginning points of the breath is not given in this meditation. Some traditions place one center in the belly and the other at the top of the head. Other traditions place the beginning points in the heart center and at a center where the outbreath ends, nine to ten inches out in front of the heart. Both ways of practicing are very effective. You may wish to try each of these and notice any difference in your experience.

Traditionally, the mantra *Hamsa* is repeated silently with the breath—*ham* on the inbreath, *sa* on the outbreath. *Hamsa* means "I am That"—with "That" referring to the true Self, divine fullness, Oneness.

Moving between two centers of focus in this meditation requires constant attention. This first meditation develops our capacity for inner focus and a heightened sense of ourselves as energy.

Breathing, centering, focusing on energy, and linking dimensions of consciousness are all woven together into one graceful and powerful meditation. Through repeated practice, this beginning meditation in either form lays a foundation for the meditations that follow.

Ultimately, this first meditation is about the dynamic energy of consciousness and its relationship to the breath. The meditation focuses on the flow of subtle energy in our body as we breathe in and out. This subtle energy, known as *prana,* is understood to be the energetic link between the physical reality and the transcendent dimension. By paying attention to this energy, we begin to access the subtler and more powerful dimensions of our consciousness from which it is easier to enter the non-dual state.

~

~

Practice crown-belly breathing

The practice of breathing between the crown of the head and the belly is an excellent preparation for many other meditations. Breathing in this way draws our attention into the energetic axis that extends like a column up the middle of the body. This has a strong centering effect, particularly when repeated for a while.

Breathing into the belly center can be challenging for some, especially at first. Many people hold a great deal of tension in the belly. Breathing into this part of the body begins to help release this tension and any corresponding emotions. With repetition, the belly center becomes a steady anchor for our vitality and instinctive self. Without this center being relaxed and energized, our spiritual development lacks a natural anchor in the physical dimension and can unfold in an ungrounded way.

- As you breathe in, the flow of energy begins at the crown of the head and flows down to the belly, just below the navel center.

- As you breathe out, the energy of the exhalation begins in the belly and rises back up to the top of the head.

- Focus on the movement of the breath and the energy in each of the two centers where the inbreath and outbreath begin.

- Let this focus take you into an awareness of the fullness of pure being.

- If you like, repeat "ham" silently on the inbreath and "sa" silently on the outbreath. After a while, you can let the mantra go and simply rest in the peaceful fullness that this meditation leads to.

~

Practice heart center breathing

The second practice of breathing between the inner heart center and the center in front of the chest where the out breath ends, draws our attention powerfully into the experience of our being as it anchors in the heart space. This heart dimension will be returned to later in the meditations.

- Feel the inbreath begin in the space in front of the chest and end in the inner space of the heart.

- Feel the outbreath start in the heart center and end in the space out in front of the body.

- Continue breathing this way, focusing on the energy in these two centers.

- The heart is the seat of the individual soul. Breathing in and out in this way, awaken to your true nature.

- If you like, you can repeat *ham* (hum) silently on the inbreath and *sa* on the outbreath. After a while, you can let the mantra go and just rest in the peaceful, awakened fullness that this meditation leads to.

2.

Pausing in the inner and outer spaces of the breath

In both the inner and outer spaces of the breath, pause. Through the great life force, pure awareness arises.

—Verse 25

In this meditation, we focus again on the two places where the breath begins, this time giving our attention to the quality of space.

When using the heart centers, the inbreath begins in the space outside the body in front of the chest and ends in the space deep inside the body. The outbreath begins in the space inside the body and ends in the space outside. As one breath ends and just before the next begins, pause for a moment in the open space.

By momentarily suspending the breath in space like this, we become more familiar with this spacious aspect of consciousness. We can begin to feel that the space outside and the space within are the same space. This is the space of the Infinite. Momentarily resting here, we can touch eternity.

The same space can be meditated on in the crown and belly centers. The following practice uses the heart spaces as its focus.

~

Practice pausing in the open spaces of the breath

- Follow the flow of the breath.
- The inbreath begins in the space outside the body and ends in the space deep inside.
- The outbreath begins in the space deep in the body and ends in the space outside.
- At the end of each breath, pause for a moment in the open space. The space outside and the space deep within are the same space. This space is the space of the Infinite, pure awareness.
- Rest in the stillness of this space and enter the eternal present.

3.
The breath rests in stillness

When the energy inherent in the breath stills, or doesn't move swiftly in any direction, it gathers in the middle. Through the dissolution of all thoughts, your amazing true nature appears.

—Verse 26

The Sanskrit word that is used to denote our "amazing true nature" is from the title of this text: *bhairava*, one of the terms this tradition uses to indicate the highest state. The word will come up many times in the verses.

The previous meditation focused on a momentary pause of the breath in the inner and outer spaces of the inhalation and exhalation. This meditation focuses on what happens as we allow that moment of pause to naturally lengthen. By focusing on the natural slowing and stilling of the breath, we enter more fully into the space of stillness. The subtle energy that moves with the breath stills as well, and now comes to rest in the subtle core of our being.

This core is experienced in our body as a central channel of subtle energy that runs from the base of the spine to the crown of the head. As the energy stills and gathers in this center, thoughts dissolve and the mind spontaneously enters the thought-free state. In this thought-free state, the spacious awareness of our true being appears.

This meditation helps us notice the relationship between the natural stilling of the breath, the gathering of energy in our core, the dissolution of thought, and the experience of the spacious awareness of our true Self. By heightening our awareness of these inner dynamics, each becomes more alive and quite naturally strengthens our experience of the other parts of this dynamic.

~

Practice resting in the breath

- As you follow your breath in meditation, allow yourself to relax more fully into the naturally occurring moments of stillness in your breathing.

- You may notice energy gathering in your core, the central column of your being.

- Notice as well that thoughts begin to dissolve.

- Even when you return to breathing, remain in the open space of the thought-free state.

- Allow the breath to continue to slow and calm on its own.

- Remain in the spacious awareness of the thought-free state, and let your true nature blossom.

4.
Retention of the breath

At the end of an inhalation or exhalation, suspend all movement of the breath and rest in tranquility. Practicing this will lead to profound peace.

—Verse 27

The first meditation in this sequence helped develop the capacity to locate and experience the energy at the beginning of each breath. The second meditation focused on pausing in the space in which each breath begins. The third meditation focused on the natural slowing of the breath as you meditate and the relationship between the stilling of the breath, the thought-free state and energy gathering in your center.

In this fourth and final meditation in the sequence, we extend the pause between the breaths by suspending all movement at the end of a full inhalation or exhalation. This longer suspension facilitates an even deeper experience. As in the previous meditation, the energy behind the movements of the breath steadies in the middle, and the mind spontaneously enters the thought-free state. In this powerful stillness, we enter fully into the peace of our true being.

To help extend the spontaneous stillness of mind that comes when suspending your breath, whenever you feel you need to breathe, it can be helpful to imagine unhooking your mind from your breath and breathing in a shallow and light manner. In this way, the movement of your breath doesn't disturb your mind's peacefulness.

~

Practice suspending the breath

- At the end of a full inhalation or exhalation, suspend all movement of your breath.

- Notice thoughts naturally dissolve in the stillness.

- Focus on the tranquility and spaciousness. Rest in the profound peace of your true nature.

- Allow the peace to continue even as the movement of the breath returns.

5.
Golden shaft in the spine

Meditate on the energy, rising up from the base of the spine like golden rays of the sun and becoming subtler and subtler until it dissolves at the crown of the head in the luminous Oneness.

—Verse 28

In the previous meditations, the currents of energy that accompany the breath have been calmed and allowed to gather into the central channel. Now, the focus shifts to the movement of this energy up the central channel along the spine and into the crown of the head. The existence of this central channel is spoken of in many spiritual traditions.

Once the energy begins to rise in that central channel, it has become a power of a higher order, known in the tradition as *kundalini*. The function of this awakened energy is to transform our consciousness, releasing us from an isolated perspective into an experience of unity with all of life.

A practice that can help us bring our awareness to this subtle level of our being is to hold the mental image of these shafts of golden light rising up through the central channel and becoming increasingly subtle until they dissolve in a field of pure light. When we focus on the sensation of light becoming ever finer, this will gradually dissolve any residual density in our awareness. Our individual sense of self can then return to its source and merge into the pure light of Consciousness.

~

Practice feeling light in the spine

- Feel or imagine a ball or sphere of energy, like the sun, at the base of your spine.

- Once this becomes palpable, feel the energy rising up your spine like a shaft of golden light emanating from the sun.

- Focus on the subtle sensation of the rising energy becoming finer and finer, gradually dissolving any residual sense of individual self until you merge at the top of your head in a field of pure light.

6.
Lightning rising in the spine sequentially

Meditate on the energy in the form of lightning, flashing upward from one energy center to another, until at last it reaches the crown of the head and the Great Dawn.

—Verse 29

The previous meditation emphasized the luminous quality of the awakened life force moving in the central channel. In this meditation the focus is on the energy's dynamic nature, the way it flashes forth.

When we concentrate on the energy surging upward in the space between each center, our awareness is drawn, vividly, into the central channel. This helps us to experience the nature of this transformative energy.

Once the energy reaches the crown of the head, any vestiges of the individual self are released. We then dissolve into the light of pure Consciousness—the light that is beautifully described here as the Great Dawn of Liberation.

The meditation traditions describe many different energy centers, known as chakras, in the subtle body. The following practice refers to the seven most widely recognized centers ascending along the central channel.

~

Practice feeling the energy flash upward

- Visualize a ball of energy at the base of your spine.

- When you have this firmly in mind, feel the energy flash like a bolt of lightning from the base center up to the second center, a few inches above it, along the spine. Feel this energy animating both centers as well as the space between them.

- Let yourself feel the energy build in the second center and then flash upward into the third center at the level of the solar plexus. Feel this energy animating both centers as well as the space in between them.

- Continue in this way, letting the energy flash between the centers near the solar plexus and the heart, the heart and throat, the throat and the point between the eyes, and the point between the eyes and the crown of the head.

- Once you reach the crown of the head, let yourself dissolve into the infinite light of Consciousness.

7.
Three levels of centers and letters

Meditate in succession on the twelve centers in the body and their corresponding letters—first at the physical level, then the subtle, and finally the transcendent—liberating each, one by one, until you become Shiva [the great ecstatic Oneness].

—Verse 30

This esoteric meditation focuses simultaneously on energy centers, vowel sounds, and subtle levels of consciousness. The great attention it requires helps develop our capacity to experience exquisite subtle inner dimensions of our consciousness.

The twelve centers, also known as the twelve stations or twelve stages of the rising kundalini, are located in the central channel along the spine. They are listed in the chart below.

The letters to be meditated on in these centers are the twelve vowels of the Sanskrit alphabet. The vowel sounds are said to be Shakti, the creative power of Consciousness.

In the accompanying table, "The chakras and their sounds," these sounds are listed in order of appearance next to the center with which each is connected.

The chakras and their sounds

ah (ah)	highest state of pure energy
am (um)	stage of pure energy
au (aou)	highest point of the cranium
o (oh)	middle of the forehead
ai (aiy)	between the eyebrows
e (eh)	top of the palate
uu (oooh)	throat
u (oo)	heart
ii (eeeh)	navel
i (ee)	between the base of spine and navel
aa (aah)	root center at the base of the spine
a (uh)	level of the perineum

At the last three stages, the energy is in its non-dual or highest form. It is no longer located in the body. The three highest stages are uniquely sublime.

~

Practice focusing on successive centers and their sounds

- In ascending sequence, repeat each vowel sound out loud, feeling it vibrate in its corresponding center in the physical body.

- In sequence, now repeat each vowel silently in your mind, feeling it vibrate in its corresponding center in the subtle energy body.

- Repeat the sequence now at the transcendent level. Begin as if you were going to say the syllable mentally in its center, but don't—and, instead, notice the place that exists before even the impulse to think arises, the transcendent level. Stay here in pure Being.

8.
Crossing the bridge

Fill the center at the roof of the mouth with energy and, with a bridge-like arch of the eyebrows, rise above all thoughts and into universal presence.

—Verse 31

The sensation of filling this esoteric center at the roof of the mouth with energy helps draw our awareness up into higher regions of our consciousness. Raising the eyebrows upward in the shape of an arch helps pull our awareness up and out of any remaining thoughts in the mind.

Freed of any last discursive activity, our awareness crosses over into the region of the crown center and into the sublime state of pure being.

~

Practice in the crown of the head

- Focus on the center at the roof of your mouth, filling it with energy.

- When ready, arch your eyebrows up in the middle.

- Let the upward movement help lift the energy out of the center and cross over into the crown region and the sublime state of universal presence.

9.
Five voids of the senses

Just as the gaze is hypnotically pulled into the dark center of the colored circles on a peacock feather, meditate in the heart on the void of the five senses until you reach the great void [the vast open space of Consciousness].

—Verse 32

The beautiful, circular configuration of a peacock feather has a hypnotic quality. The compelling beauty of the concentric circles surrounding the feather's dark center can help pull our awareness away from our five senses and plunge it deep into the exquisite velvet blackness of the causal level in the heart. Meditating on this black center in the heart helps to draw us into the void, the open space of limitless Consciousness from where all creation emanates.

This meditation is an elegant form of sense withdrawal (*pratyahara*), a well-known practice where, in preparation for meditation, our attention is completely withdrawn from the senses and brought back to the center of our being.

The Sanskrit term *"shunya,"* which appears in this meditation, is often translated in this tradition as "void." Other traditions translate it as "emptiness." Although the term comes up often in many Eastern philosophical traditions, Westerners can be disoriented by either of these ways of interpreting *shunya*. Thinking of this as "space" is an easier way for some people to approach the sublime state that the term points to. In the practice below, you might want to experiment with each of the terms—void, emptiness, space—and notice any difference in your experience.

~

Practice meditating on the void

- Imagine looking at the beautiful concentric circles of a peacock feather.

- In the same way that you can be hypnotically pulled into the dark center of this feather, meditate on the velvet darkness of the void in the center of your heart.

10.
Mindful concentration on a peaceful object

In the same way, wherever there is mindful awareness, whether on a void, a wall, or an excellent person, gradually, the boon of merging into the Self is attained.

—Verse 33

The conscious engagement of life experience in all its forms lies at the heart of this path. This meditation gives a variety of examples of what can be used as a meditative focus to help shift us into awareness of the ultimate source—from the subtle emptiness of the void to a steadying object like a wall and the inspiring qualities of a highly evolved person. With such varied examples, there is an indication that anything peaceful in the entire world can be used for meditation.

In the previous meditation, the mindful focus was solely on a deep inner reality. In this meditation, our mindful focus is on the void or on objects in our outer reality. The author is pointing out that whether our attention is on our inner or outer reality, it leads to the same state of Oneness.

~

Practice calming the mind

- Choose something in life that naturally calms your mind or inspires you—such as an open space, someone you love, or something you find beautiful.

- Concentrate on this person, place, or object, allowing its natural peaceful qualities to help still your mind and bring it to a single focus.

- Stay with this mindful awareness and gradually merge back into your true Self.

11.
The interior of the cranium

Focus on the interior of the crown of your skull. As your mind steadies here, direct your attention toward the highest principle that can be discerned—which will gradually become discernible!

—Verse 34

This meditation continues to engage our inner senses, our ability to feel and see at the subtle level. The instruction to focus on the interior of the skull anchors the extremely subtle experience of the crown center into the solid bone of the body. By steadying our attention here, at the body's highest center of Consciousness, the last vestiges of our sense of individuality gradually merge into Oneness.

In the verse's second line, the instruction to focus on the highest principle that can be discerned engages the most subtle aspects of our intuition.

The experience of this highest center in the body often appears initially as a field of light. Yogis call this luminous energy the light of a thousand suns. All physical dimensions dissolve at this level. We enter the Oneness.

~

Practice focusing on the crown of the head

- Focus your attention on the interior of the crown of your skull. Notice the sensations here.

- Gradually, become aware of the exquisite subtle energy in the crown of your head. Become steady in this experience.

- As the teeming, pulsing energy of the great, embracing Oneness becomes more palpable, allow yourself to merge into it.

12.
Inner space of the inner axis

The central channel in the middle is slender, like a single fiber of a lotus stalk. Meditate on the subtle space within the fiber, and through the grace of the life energy, the Infinite will be revealed.

—Verse 35

A fiber of a lotus stalk is as thin as a thread. The idea of trying to enter into something so thin pushes us to discover how to readjust our attention to penetrate into such a tiny dimension. This is not as unfamiliar an idea as we might think. Folklore, literature, and poetry have always had references to this capacity. For example, from William Blake:

> To see a World in a Grain of Sand
> And a Heaven in a Wild Flower,
> Hold Infinity in the palm of your hand
> And Eternity in an hour.

Once we discover how to enter into the threadlike thinness of the central channel, which can feel like shrinking ourselves down infinitesimally in order to enter this dimension, then the instruction to focus on the space *within* this tininess precipitates yet another shift in dimension—that of opening into spaciousness within something infinitely small.

These shifts in dimension help loosen our habitual identification with our ego and body and move us past the boundaries of the personal physical level and into the subtle and beyond.

~

Practice meditating on the central channel

- To support yourself in feeling the central channel, imagine the left and right sides of your body as two separate halves. Then bring these two halves together, focusing on the felt sense of where they are joined.

- Now, meditate on the central channel as a thread of exquisite energy running from the base of your spine up to the crown of your head.

- Imagine that you are entering into the threadlike channel itself. In your own time, tune into the sensation of the subtle space within the channel and allow the subtle energy in the space to take you into the Infinite.

13.
Point of light

Block all the openings of the head with the fingers, and focus intently at the center between the eyebrows. Once the psychic knot here is pierced, an exquisite point of pure light gradually appears. Become absorbed in the shimmering light, and merge into the sublime.

—Verse 36

The center between the eyebrows is called the *ajna chakra* and also the eye of unity. The opening of this center and its accompanying extraordinary shift of perception is spoken of in many spiritual traditions. There is a knot of nerves at this center, and piercing this knot provides entry into higher states of consciousness. It can take some time for the energy to build to a strong enough level to break though the knot.

In this meditation we help the energy to gather by blocking the openings of the head. We do this by closing them off manually with our fingers. This inhibits the natural outflow of energy. The hand position blocking the openings of the head, which is described in the practice below, is known as *shanmukhi mudra* and serves to remind us to withdraw all the outgoing energy of our senses and to direct this energy back within to its source. In this case, we are directing the energy toward the eyebrow center.

As this center begins to open, some people experience a subtle field of light or energy; others, a brilliant point of light. By continuing to meditate on this light, we eventually merge into the light and the state of pure being.

Many people find that this powerful meditation works when they omit the hand gesture and focus directly on the point between the eyebrows.

~

Practice with a point of light

- Begin by placing the thumbs in the ears, the index fingers over the eyes, the middle fingers on the nostrils, the ring fingers above the lips, and the little fingers below the lips. (This symbolic hand gesture helps remind us to withdraw all outgoing energy from our senses and to hold that energy within, allowing it to return to its source. The traditional image is of a turtle, pulling its limbs inside its shell.)

- Direct all your energy up to the center just above the middle of your eyebrows. To help focus the energy in this center, you may find it helpful to visualize a bright point of light.

- As you continue directing energy into this center, gradually, a natural point of light, or field of light, will appear.

- Meditate on this light, merging into it and the state of pure being.

14.
The flame in the heart

When the eyes are rubbed, sparks of light appear. Meditate on a spark of light like this or on a steady flame in your heart or at the top of your head—and dissolve into the great light of Consciousness.

—Verse 37

In spiritual traditions throughout the ages, light has always been seen as a powerful, universal symbol of the highest states of Consciousness, the Divine. Here, a spark of light or a steady flame is to be meditated on either in the heart center or at the crown of the head. This image of a single point of radiant luminosity in the open space of our awareness is both beautiful and hypnotic. Focusing on this point of light draws our mind to a single point of focus and, through this focus, we can penetrate the shimmering light and merge into the luminous field of pure Consciousness.

Notice that several options are given in this meditation—a spark or a flame, in our heart space or at crown of the head. These are all wonderful possibilities for focus. You might try experimenting with each and note any differences in your experience.

Notice, too, how in many of these *Vijnana Bhairava* meditations, simple human experiences that are part of our daily lives—in this instance, the sparks we see when rubbing our eyes or the flame we might see on a candle—are used as doorways into the Infinite.

~

Practice meditating on light

- Meditate on a spark of light or a steady flame in your heart or at the crown of your head.

- Become completely absorbed in this luminous, shimmering point, and dissolve into the infinite light of Consciousness.

15.
The unstruck sounds within

Listen to the subtle inner sounds that are not caused by any external source and are continuous, like the roar of a waterfall. Become adept at merging in these manifestations of the Infinite in the form of sound, and you will become the Infinite.

—Verse 38

The practice of meditating on inner sounds is an ancient and much-loved practice in the East. If we take a moment and listen very carefully, we can begin to hear a high-pitched ringing in the ear. This continuous ringing happens on its own, as do all the inner sounds referred to in this meditation.

In the yogic tradition, these sounds are known as unstruck sounds because, unlike the physical sounds we hear, these inner sounds are not created by the striking of one object against another—wind on vocal cords, hammer on wood, water on rocks. These subtle sounds arise from within us on their own.

Many yogic texts give extensive lists of the subtle inner sounds. These include sounds such as the high-pitched ringing of tiny cymbals, crickets at night, tiny bells tinkling continuously, and the low roar of distant thunder. These subtle sounds can be heard when we become quiet and focus on the inner world of vibration.

The entire universe is energy vibrating in an infinite number of patterns. Focusing on one of these inner vibrations helps tune our mind to the subtle inner world. As we become more familiar with these subtle sounds, we can merge into them and let them carry us back into the Oneness from which all vibrations arise.

~

Practice with the subtle sounds

- Begin to listen to the subtle inner world of vibration. Be open and curious. As your mind quiets, it becomes easier to start to hear these inner vibrations, which often sound like subtle forms of outer sounds.

- Concentrate on one of the subtle inner sounds, such as a high-pitched ringing, crickets at night, tiny bells tinkling, the humming of bees, the sound of a waterfall, or the low roar of distant thunder.

- Become adept at merging into whichever inner sound you are most drawn to. Allow this sound to take you into the Oneness.

16.
Void at the end of *Om*

Chanting *Om* perfectly, meditate on the emptiness at the very end of its lingering reverberation. The transcending energy of this seeming emptiness will take you into the great all-embracing void itself.

—Verse 39

Om is considered the primordial sound, the first sound of creation. In this meditation we follow its sound all the way to its last lingering reverberations and into the vast space of emptiness where it dissolves.

This vast emptiness, a seeming void, is full of energy—the same creative energy that pervades and creates universes. As we become aware of this exquisite energy and learn how to enter into it, the energy itself will take us into that which is empty of all differentiation, into pure being.

Chanting *Om* perfectly here means pronouncing it as described in the practice below.

~

Practice with *Om*

- Chant the sound *Om* fully, pronouncing each of its three syllables—*ah, uu, mm*—and lingering on the final *mm* as it dissolves into pure space at the very end.

- Notice that this ultimate emptiness is free of all objects but teeming with the energy of Consciousness.

- Rest in the emptiness and allow the sublime energy here to take you into the Oneness.

17.
Void behind the letters

Think deeply about the condition of a letter before or after it is spoken as being empty. Through the power of this nothingness, become one with the vastness of pure awareness.

—Verse 40

Everything in life appears out of the formless One and, in its own time, returns to this Oneness. If we consider any letter of any alphabet and notice the formless condition this letter exists in, both before and after it is spoken, this practice will help us to feel the spacious emptiness, the void from which all things arise and to which they return.

This formless aspect of universal Consciousness, the One, pulsates with the creative universal power. Once we have noticed this, if we focus our attention on the creative energy, that very energy will take us into the vastness of the great void.

The practice below works with the letter "*a*" as an example of how this meditation can be approached.

~

Practice with the letters

- Contemplate the letter "*a.*" Let yourself feel where this letter exists before you say or even think it. Stay there in this place of seeming nothingness, which is the letter's source. The letter exists in the same void condition after you have said it.

- Think or say aloud the letter "*a.*"

- Let yourself feel into where this sound or thought has gone. Stay there.

- As you continue to focus on this void, with the help of the great energy of this extraordinary state, you will become one with the nature and vastness of the great void.

18.
The end of a musical sound

With one-pointed awareness, listen to the prolonged sound of a musical instrument right to the sound's very end and its gradual dissolution into the great space of Consciousness.

—Verse 41

This simple, elegant meditation on sound is one of many meditations in the text based in our common daily experience. Although this meditation speaks specifically of the sounds of musical instruments, the text is capturing something that is a universal experience. Almost everyone has at some time or another been transported into a thought-free state by hearing a train whistle or a foghorn dissolve into the night.

This meditation is also a favorite in the Zen tradition, where the sound of a gong is purposely followed into the space of emptiness. One way to practice this on your own is to ring a gong or chime and listen to the sound as it finally fades right into the Infinite.

~

Practice with a prolonged sound

- Follow any prolonged sound as it becomes subtler and subtler, right to its very end, where it dissolves in the great space of Consciousness.

19.
Seed mantras into emptiness

Meditate on the seed mantras (*a, aa, i, ii... aum, aim, hrim...*) and on their progressively subtler levels of vibration, ending in the source emptiness that is Shiva [supremely free Consciousness].

—Verse 42

This meditation is a beautiful example of moving our attention from the physical to the subtle and then into the emptiness of pure Consciousness, known in this tradition as Shiva. Each seed sound has its own power, and this power becomes stronger as we penetrate closer to its source. The pure emptiness at the sound's core is a doorway into our Shiva nature, supremely free Consciousness.

Seed sounds commonly used for meditation include the vowel sounds of the Sanskrit alphabet (*a, aa, i, ii*, and so on), and seed sounds from the energy traditions (*aim, hreem, kleem, shreem, ha, ham, ksham, and so on*). The practice below employs the seed sound *ha*.

~

Practice with seed mantras

- Repeat the seed mantra *ha* aloud.

- Now, repeat it silently in your mind. (This is the subtle level.)

- Finally, begin to think the sound, but don't. Notice where even the impulse to think comes from. Stay here and allow yourself to merge into the Infinite.

20.
Emptiness all around, simultaneously

Contemplate that your body is nothing but space in all directions simultaneously. Your mind will become free of thoughts, and you will become infinitely spacious.

—Verse 43

This is the first of a series of meditations introducing us to the extraordinary experience of *bhairavi mudra,* where our awareness is centered deeply within and simultaneously extended outward in all directions. The thought of the body being empty or pure space dissolves our sense of the body's physical boundaries. This, in turn, frees our awareness to extend out in all directions into the space that surrounds us.

In this meditation, we begin with the physical body and hold to the thought that the body is pure emptiness in all directions, rather than moving step by step through the physical, subtle and transcendent levels. This sudden approach catapults us beyond thought constructs, helping us learn how to flex our consciousness in a new way. At the same time, the meditation reinforces how close we actually are to the experience of Oneness.

Before you begin this meditation, it can be helpful to first practice by becoming aware of the space in front of the body. Wait for a felt sense of this space. Then extend your awareness to feel the space behind your body. Again, wait until you feel this. Then, in the same way, feel out into the space to the left and the right sides, and then above and below. Once you have a felt sense of the various directions, center yourself, gather the energy, and then begin the practice.

~

Practice with the notion of space

- Hold firm to the idea that your body is nothing but space in all directions simultaneously.

- Notice how your thoughts recede as you enter the powerful, direct experience of the infinitely spacious present moment.

21.
Simultaneous space at crown and base

Meditate simultaneously on the space above the head and space at the base of the spine. Through the sublime energy of this state, you become one with the infinite space of Consciousness.

—Verse 44

The rational mind can focus on only one thing at a time. Focusing simultaneously on two different places pushes us beyond the mind and into pure awareness, which can hold things simultaneously.

This is the first of many meditations that begin with a dual focus—two thoughts, two objects, two experiences—and instruct us to hold both in our mind until the tension causes a shift into pure awareness. In this tradition, the Sanskrit term for the awareness that is found in between two things is *madhya,* which means, literally, "the middle" and is frequently translated as the "heart" or "center." It is another name for the Self, our true nature.

The term *shunya* in the original text is being rendered here as "space," for the same reasons given in the commentary on meditation 9.

~

Practice with space in crown and base

- Meditate on the space above your head and the space at the base of your spine simultaneously.

- Feel the quality of space in both places.

- Let yourself dissolve into the vast space of pure awareness.

22.
Space at the crown, base, and heart

Meditate simultaneously on the space above [the crown of the head], the space at the base [of the spine], and the space in the heart. The mind becomes free of all fluctuations and the great thought-free state arises.

—Verse 45

Adding the heart as a third point of focus short-circuits any remaining mental activity and catapults us further into the thought-free state. Also, including the heart center helps bring the experience of empty spaciousness more fully into our body. Feeling yourself as space, as pure emptiness, is the same as feeling yourself as pure being. Focusing on space is simply another way of approaching the experience of Oneness.

~

Practice with space in crown, base and heart

- Meditate simultaneously on space above your head, space at the base of the spine, and space in the heart.

- As your mind becomes free of thoughts, rest in the vastness.

23.
The body as space

Concentrate on your body as pure space with a mind free of thoughts for even a moment, and that sublime thought-free state will become your very reality.

—Verse 46

After repeatedly fixing our attention in the previous three meditations on space—on the emptiness, the void—the beloved thought-free state that accompanies this experience begins to become more familiar. The text is reminding us—as it will do many times again—that once we understand a classical principle behind a means of meditation, even the tiniest remembrance of this principle can help us shift almost instantly into the awakened state.

Rather than asking us to control our thoughts, the instructions pair our focus on the subtle experience of emptiness with the experience of the thought-free state of mind. Focusing on our body as pure emptiness helps dissolve the sense of being a solid, separate, isolated self. It is the sense of solidness and separation that drives so much of our reactive thinking. Dissolving the sense of our body's solidity can be a helpful and gentle way to go beyond the grip of our thoughts.

~

Practice with the body as space

- Think of your entire body as being void or empty or nothing but space.

- Hold this experience without forming any thoughts about the experience or anything else.

- Notice how easily you can become one with the great state beyond all thought.

24.
Constituents of the body as void

Dear One, focus on the various parts of the body—such as the flesh, muscles, organs, or bones—as being empty, nothing but space. Your contemplation of the great spaciousness will become unshakable.

—Verse 47

Meditating on our flesh, muscles, organs, or bones as being empty brings our awareness even more deeply into the body, further grounding our experience of the emptiness that is the source of all things.

Notice that in these meditations we are not being asked to transcend our body. We are using our physical experience as the starting place from which to enter into the experience of transcendence. Focusing on emptiness while deep in our flesh, muscles, organs and bones helps us ground our attention into the body while simultaneously releasing any limiting density associated with the separate sense of self. This approach helps integrate all levels of our being in the experience of Oneness.

~

Practice on body constituents as void

- Close your eyes and focus on the physical sensations of your body.

- Let your awareness flow down into the body from your head so that you begin to feel from within the body rather than looking down at the body from your head.

- In your own time, tune into the sensations of the flesh, muscles, organs, and bones of your body, contemplating that each of these is, at a deeper level, empty—nothing but pure, open space.

- Stay with this feeling of emptiness from within your body and let the feeling itself take you into the great space that contains all things.

25.
The body merely as skin, covering void

Meditate on your body as pure space bounded by a thin covering of skin and become that state which cannot be meditated on!

—Verse 48

This meditation combines the sensation of emptiness in the body with the sensation of the boundary of our skin. Again, we are not transcending the body. Rather, we are using our experience of the body to help us merge into the non-dual experience, where the physical and the formless are all part of the same Oneness.

This is the first of many meditations that focuses on a pairing of opposites—in this case emptiness and a tactile boundary. This focus on two things simultaneously helps precipitate a shift into pure awareness where our normal sense of separation dissolves.

The second line of the verse is making a playful but exalted philosophical point—that the state of pure awareness this meditation leads to can be experienced only by becoming that awareness. In the state of Oneness, there is no separate self left to meditate on anything!

This is a sublime meditation. The sensation of inner space bounded by a thin covering of skin can be exquisitely subtle and sensual. As unusual as this instruction sounds, many beginners find this meditation quite easy to imagine and experience.

~

Practice with the body as skin covering space

- Close your eyes and let yourself feel that your body is nothing but space covered by a thin boundary of skin.
- Stay with this sensation until all boundaries dissolve.

26.
The bowls of the heart

Focus on the space within the two bowls of the heart center with one-pointed concentration. You will become the embodiment of good fortune.

—Verse 49

To continue to help us embody the experience of space (or the void) as a quality of our essential Self, we are instructed to focus on the sensation of space right in the middle of our heart center.

The heart center is understood in this tradition to be the seat of the individual soul, and so it is given an incredibly important place. To help us experience our heart center, we are given the image of the heart space as being contained between two bowls, one inverted over the other forming a sphere. In one tradition, these bowls are described as golden. The image of the two golden bowls is quite beautiful, and it sets up a powerful tactile sensation that can help pull us into the extraordinary experience.

~

Practice focusing on the bowls of the heart

- Visualize two golden bowls, one inverted over the other, right in the center of your chest. Stay with the beautiful visual and tactile qualities of these two golden bowls.

- Allow your attention to be drawn deeply into the space of your heart. Enter into the space contained in between the two bowls and rest here.

27.
Consciousness fills the body, the mind dissolves in the center

With your awareness pervading your entire body, dissolve your mind right in the center of the heart. With steady attention and steady practice, your true Self will appear.

—Verse 50

As in many of the previous meditations, we begin here with the body as our focus. First, we allow our awareness to spread throughout the entire body. Then, while maintaining this awareness, we dissolve our mind in the middle of the heart center. The combination of spacious, embodied awareness and a penetrating focus on the heart keeps us grounded in our body while simultaneously taking us beyond the mind and into pure being.

This heart meditation emphasizes the value of steady practice.

~

Practice focusing on the center of the heart

- Let your awareness fill your entire body.
- Once this feeling is steady, focus your mind in the center of your heart and allow the mind to dissolve into the Oneness.

28.
Fixing attention again and again on the heart

Throw your mind into your heart center again and again, wherever you are, in whatever way you can! The fluctuations of your mind will begin to calm and, within a few days, you will achieve an extraordinary state.

—Verse 51

The two previous meditations recommended entering the heart through one-pointed concentration (#26) and through regular practice (#27). This meditation emphasizes a constant repetition of short, focused bursts of attention—at any time and in any way!

This last instruction captures the profoundly life-embracing stance of this tradition. We will see more of this irrepressibly positive and joyous approach as the text unfolds.

~

Practice being in the heart all the time

- At any time of the day, in any circumstance, and in whatever way works best for you, throw your mind into your heart, over and over again!

- Make being in your heart more important than anything else, until living from your heart becomes your default position, and you are living every moment of life from your heart.

29.
The fire of time

Contemplate the great consuming quality of the movement of time as a fire rising upward inside you, consuming your entire body. At the end of this meditation, you will experience a great tranquility.

—Verse 52

Nothing is permanent. Time eventually consumes all things in the universe, freeing them from their form and returning them to their source, which is pure being. Since our physical body is the anchor for our sense of our limited, separate self, by imagining that our body is being consumed by the metaphoric fire of time, we are freed of our sense of limitation, making it easier for us to release into pure being.

Over the years many great philosophers have encouraged us to meditate on the transient nature of life and the inevitability of our own death to help us find what is truly meaningful. In this meditation, we engage the image of fire to help us focus on the powerful energetic nature of a seemingly destructive event. The very intensity of our contemplation propels us into freedom.

One translation of this meditation instructs us to begin by visualizing this fire of time *(kalagni)* as being in our right big toe. As unusual as it may seem, this focus is effective in grounding this powerful meditation in the body.

~

Practice visualizing your body in flames

- Visualize the all-consuming fire of time, beginning in the big toe of your right foot. Watch this flame rise upward until it consumes your entire body.

- As the last vestiges of your body fall away, rest in great tranquility.

30.
The fire of time burns the world

With a one-pointed and undisturbed mind, contemplate the whole world being consumed by the fire of time. The highest state will dawn.

—Verse 58

The previous meditation used the image of our body being consumed by the fire of time to help us release our sense of being a separate individual, which is anchored in the body. In this meditation, we contemplate the fire of time consuming the whole outer world to help us dissolve the apparent sense of solidity and separation that is inherent in our everyday perception of the world around us.

As we remember that the whole world will disappear at some point, our ego relaxes and we begin to remember the eternal dimensions of our true Self.

~

Practice visualizing the world in flames

- Steady yourself and contemplate the entire world being consumed by the fire of time.

- Remember that everything that exists will, at some point, return to its formless source.

- As the apparent solidity of the world falls away—taking with it everything that we worry about—the timeless dimensions of reality dawn.

31.
Dissolving the principles of manifestation

Meditate on the constitutive principles of your body or of the world—from the physical to the subtle to the very subtlest, dissolving each into its respective cause. This ends in the supreme source of existence.

—Verse 54

Each of the philosophies and religions in the world has its own way of approaching the various levels of creation. Some have just one principle: the material universe. Some have two: human and God, the individual and the universal. Some use three basic principles, such as body, mind, and spirit or physical, subtle, and universal. Others have as many as thirty-six principles.

The beauty of this particular meditation is that, once the idea of dissolving a denser level into the next subtler level starts becoming familiar, it can be applied to any of these descriptions of creation. For example, we already instinctively dissolve one level into the next higher level when we notice we are stuck in a thought or emotion and choose to "lighten up" and move on.

It is possible to experience the power of this meditation by choosing any gradations of consciousness with which you are familiar.

The following practice uses the final five elements of the Shaivite principles of creation—those that correspond with the physical elements. Many people find themselves in a powerful state of awareness at the end of working with just these five principles of materiality—earth, water, fire, air, and ether (space)—letting each one dissolve into the next subtler element.

~

Practice meditating on the physical elements

- Begin with the earth principle, bringing images of earth to mind—a sandy beach, soil in your garden, a mountain. Allow as many different images of earth to come up as you can. Linger with the ones that feel most vivid to you. You are tuning into the earth principle.

- When you're ready, let the feeling of earth dissolve into water, the next subtler principle of creation. Allow different images of water to come to mind—perhaps an ocean, a river, a waterfall, a dew drop, a pool of rain. Enter fully into the feeling of each image. This is the water principle.

- When you're ready, let the feeling of water dissolve into the vibration of fire and light. Let as many images of fire and light come to mind as you can. Enter into each one, feeling it fully.

- When you're ready, let the vibration of fire dissolve into air, different images of air—a high wind, a gentle summer breeze, the cool night air…Linger with the feeling of each of these.

- When you're ready, let the sense of air dissolve into images and experiences of the ether, of space. Allow yourself to tune into this, the subtlest of the elements. Space permeates everything. Let yourself begin to see and feel the space in which everything, including the universe, appears—how exquisitely subtle yet palpable it is. Rest in this feeling.

32.
From the physical to the subtle breath, in the heart

Meditate on the physical and subtle levels of the breath in the space of the heart, dissolving the inner senses and the notion of a separate self. You will become liberated from the dream of separation.

—Verse 55

This meditation introduces another practice of dissolving the levels of manifestation to become free of their binding qualities and to return to the non-dual state of Oneness. Here, we focus in the heart center, first on the physical and then on the subtle levels of the breath. The meditation pulls our awareness deep inside from where it is easier to feel, and then begin to release, the limiting dynamics of the inner senses, the individual mind, and the ego sense.

Taking the help of the subtle movement of the breath, we focus on dissolving the density of these inner principles until we can be fully free of them and can step into the limitless expanse of our true nature.

~

Practice focusing on the breath— physical and subtle

- Become aware of the physical sensation of your breath as it flows in and out.

- Focus on the sensation of this physical level of your breath now in the space of your heart.

- Feel this physical breath begin to dissolve the binding density of your senses and your sense of being a separate self.

- Gradually, become aware of the subtle level of the breath and the refined energetic sensations that accompany the breath in your heart, allowing it to continue dissolving any remaining density of the inner senses, lower mind, and separate "I" sense.

33.
Dissolving the levels of the universe

Meditate on the universe and its evolution through time and space, gradually dissolving the physical into the subtle level and the subtle into the transcendent until your mind dissolves.

—Verse 56

Here, we meditate on the course of the evolution of the universe through time and space, reversing the order of creation by gradually moving our awareness from the physical level, to the subtle level, and then all the way back to the source, prior to creation. The experience becomes increasingly more subtle and finally the mind dissolves as well, and all that is left is the experience of pure Consciousness.

This meditation begins with our focus on the physical aspects of the universe. Once this is fully and vividly present for our senses, we then shift our attention to the subtle or energetic level of reality. Just knowing that there *is* a subtle energetic dimension to the world we usually perceive helps us begin to engage our contemplative mind and the inner senses that are able to tune into this level of reality.

This energetic experience of reality requires an extension of our awareness into this dimension. As we begin to experience reality at this level, our corresponding sense of self becomes less dense as well; it becomes intermingled with what we are experiencing. We begin to feel a sense of being a part of what ordinarily appears to us as separate, as being other than us.

From this perspective, we then meditate directly on the unity of all that exists. As we do this, our individual sense of self gradually dissolves into the experience of Oneness. We are in the non-dual state of pure awareness and being, a state in which there is no longer any separation from what we experience.

74

This meditation can be done with the eyes open as a direct seeing exercise or as a contemplative exercise with the eyes closed.

~

Practice dissolving the levels of the universe

- Contemplate the physical universe and its extraordinary manifest nature. Engage all of your physical senses. Let yourself experience the immensity.

- Once you're ready, shift your attention to the subtle, energetic level of what appears as physical reality. Feel the dreamlike nature of this dimension, where time and space soften and become more fluid, where energy is pulsing and undulating in and out of fields of potential.

- Hold this focus until your intuitive perception of this dimension and your corresponding inner senses begin to engage, allowing you to experience the universe at this level.

- Let your awareness extend out into this dimension. Notice the softening and dissolving of your separate sense of self as you begin to intermingle with your experience of the subtle world of energy.

- When you're ready, penetrate even more deeply into your experience until you touch the dimension of pure being. All sense of separation and differentiation dissolve here into the sublime, non-dual Oneness.

34.
Travel back in creation to before time

Using the previous meditation on the physical, subtle, and transcendent levels to arrive at the highest Consciousness, contemplate that sublime principle as being present in all directions and at every level of the universe.

—Verse 57

In this meditation, we take the exquisite sense of Oneness that we arrived at in the last meditation and then contemplate that principle as being present in all directions and in all dimensions of the universe.

We become anchored in pure being and then feel that same experience to be present in all directions and in all dimensions of reality. This is a powerful and beautiful way of engaging the non-dual state in which we experience no difference between the being in ourselves and the being in what we perceive.

The beauty of these meditations is that they begin to blend into each other like great rivers merging, carrying everything back to the same one source.

~

Practice being the universe

- Meditate on the physical and subtle levels of the universe until you arrive at the experience of pure being.

- Once your awareness is steady in the feeling of pure being, contemplate this sublime principle as being present in all directions and in all dimensions of the universe. The being in you is the same being that is in all things in the universe. You and the universe are one. You are the universe.

35.
The universe as void

Concentrate on the thought that the entire universe is totally empty. As you focus on this vast emptiness, your mind will dissolve and then so will you!

—Verse 58

In this meditation, instead of contemplating the universe as full of being, of Oneness, we are guided to concentrate on it as being completely empty of any content. This takes our awareness to the causal level, the seeming emptiness that exists prior to any form.

The great Christian mystic Meister Eckhart called these two approaches the *via positiva* and the *via negativa*—the path of affirming that the Oneness is all things and the path of asserting that it is no nameable thing. In this meditation, with no content to focus on, our mind dissolves and with it our sense of being separate from the universe.

~

Practice on the universe as void

- Concentrate on the thought that the whole universe is empty: no thought, no image, no form, no place, no time, no body, no one, no universe.

- Focus on this emptiness. Your mind will gradually dissolve and along with it the last vestiges of your individual self.

36.
The space in a jar

Steadily gaze into the empty space inside a jar. Then, leave aside the enclosing walls and let your mind merge at once into the remaining empty space and become absorbed in the formless space of Consciousness.

—Verse 59

With this meditation comes the first of many shifts that occur throughout the text, moving from a focus that is vast and esoteric to one that is utterly mundane. Focusing on the space or emptiness inside a jar—or a cup or any open container—brings the previous abstraction of the infinite universe into the personal, physical realm. The text helps us weave together the two seemingly divergent realities of the Infinite and the personal, of being serious and being playful.

This is the first of the many fully open-eyed meditations that will appear throughout the text.

~

Practice with an empty container

- Steadily gaze into the empty space inside any open container, like a jar or a cup.

- Then, imagine letting the enclosing walls fall away so that nothing but space remains. Let your mind merge into the space.

- Stay with this feeling of merging with the space until your individual self has merged into the vastness of the Infinite.

37.
The supportless nature of a treeless mountain

Gaze steadily at a mountain free of trees. With no objects for the mind to dwell on, thoughts naturally fall away, and the mind dissolves.

—Verse 60

The majestic beauty of a barren mountain makes it another natural gateway into the Infinite. Without any objects, such as trees, for the mind to dwell upon, our awareness expands to include the experience as a whole. In this meditation, the goal is described in terms of the dissolution of the mind—the state in which there is direct and immediate contact with life without seeing it through the filter of thoughts.

The focus on space within a cup in the last meditation has been expanded in this meditation to the spacious beauty of a mountain.

~

Practice with a bare mountain

- When you come across a bare mountain, pause for a moment and gaze steadily at it.

- As thoughts naturally fall away, stay with the feeling of the open space, dissolving your mind into the vastness.

38.
The gap between two thoughts or objects—throw both away

Focus your mind on any two objects or mental states and then become aware of the space in the middle. As your awareness of this middle space steadies, let go of the two objects simultaneously, and the truth will flash forth!

—Verse 61

This is a much-loved practice in this tradition. The mind cannot hold two points simultaneously within its focus. The very act of trying to focus on two points at once precipitates a shift into a unique and relaxed state of awareness that is capable of holding multiple perceptions simultaneously. (This practice was introduced in meditation 22, where we focused on emptiness at both the top and base of our spine.)

In this meditation to help us enter the spontaneous nature of the middle space, we choose two objects of focus and then put our attention on the space between them. These two objects are held in our awareness to help stabilize our attention around the space.

As you start to feel the quality of the space between the objects, there comes a moment when you drop the objects and plunge into the space of non-conceptual awareness.

The Sanskrit term for this space of pure awareness that can be found in the middle, between two things, is *madhya*. This is one of those marvelously rich words that has multiple meanings and, often, multiple levels within each of those meanings. Simply said, at the physical level, this term means "the middle" or "the space between two things." At the subtle level, it can refer to the heart center, the seat of the individual soul. And at the highest level, it refers to "pure being," the universal Self. In these meditations, *madhya* is to be understood on all three levels at once.

Here, we begin with the physical level and then allow ourselves to penetrate into the subtle and non-dual levels of meaning in steps. This practice can also be employed with any two mental states—waking and dreaming, confusion and clarity, anger and peace, and so on. The following practice involves a focus on two physical objects.

~

Practice with the space between

- Take any two objects in your field of vision and focus on both. Have a clear intention allowing your mind to feel its way into this dual focus.

- Then, keeping both objects in your awareness, focus on the space in between the two objects.

- Once your awareness of the middle space has steadied, simultaneously let go of both objects—and enjoy the flash of non-dual awareness!

39.
Leave one object, don't move to the next

When your mind leaves one object, firmly restrain it, not allowing it to go on to another object. In the feeling of this space, awareness blossoms.

—Verse 62

It is the nature of the mind to continually move from one object to another. By pausing for a moment at the end of attending to one thing and not rushing on to the next, we interrupt the constant movement of our mind. Our attention is momentarily free to notice the pure awareness, our true Self, that has always been present, as if in the background, affectionately observing the self-luminous screen on which all our life experiences appear.

The object in question may be anything: a physical object, a sensory experience, a thought, a moment of time, a state of mind… It can be anything at all that has become the primary object of our attention. As our attention leaves this object, we are to hold firmly in the space that appears without moving on to the next object: the next breath, the next sip of coffee, the next thought… Instead, we are to enter into the space of this timeless moment where non-dual awareness is waiting for us.

The following practice employs a physical object, but bear in mind that anything the mind can focus on can be used here.

~

Practice staying in the space between

- Focus clearly on an object in your field of vision.

- Once your mind is ready to move on to another object, notice the pull to move, but don't let that happen.

- Stay right in the space after the first object and before the next.

- Timeless awareness blossoms.

40.
All is Consciousness

With an unwavering mind, hold steady to the thought that your body and the entire universe are simultaneously nothing but Consciousness. A divine state will arise.

—Verse 63

This meditation is the first of many that will approach reality directly through one powerful thought: *all is Consciousness.* True to the non-dual approach, the body and the world are not to be transcended here but to be seen for what they truly are—nothing but expressions of the same one reality.

As with many of the previous meditations, we are asked to hold two objects in our awareness—this time, the apparent opposite perspectives of our body and the universe. We enter into the heart of the meditation by focusing on the powerful thought that these are nothing but the same Consciousness.

Here, the term "simultaneous" implies action that takes place "suddenly" as well as action that involves more than one object "all at once." This is a classic meditation in which the tension of apparent opposites is used to penetrate into the experience of the great unifying Oneness. It is best approached by gathering our thoughts and energy and then entering into it with a sudden burst of focus.

~

Practice thinking, "all is Consciousness"

- Hold firmly to the thought that both your body and the entire universe are simultaneously nothing but Consciousness.

41.
Fusion of the breaths

Let the inbreath merge into the outbreath, and the outbreath merge into the inbreath. In the place where the breaths merge, in or out, you will experience knowing the great equality.

—Verse 64

In this meditation, we continue with the practice of holding two objects in our attention to help precipitate a shift into the middle state, our center. In this case the objects are the currents of breath, coming in and going out of the body.

Here, we enter the center, our true Self, by experiencing the merging of the flow of one breath into the flow of the next breath. This is impossible at the physical level, so as we try to sense this, our awareness spontaneously shifts to the subtle energetic level where—like waves or currents of water merging—we can, indeed, feel this fusion take place. The sensation of the energy currents merging into one another can carry us into a state beyond thought. For many, this is felt as a profound stillness or a sense of fullness in which the intuitive experience of the equality of all things naturally arises.

This meditation is very kinetic and sensory. It returns to the breath techniques presented in the beginning and weaves them together with the holding of two objects and the idea of merging in the center.

~

Practice fusing the breaths

- Follow the flow of your breath.
- Feel the end of the inbreath merge into the beginning of the outbreath, and the end of the outbreath merge into the beginning of the inbreath.
- In the places where the two breaths merge—whether this is in your heart center or in the outer space in front—let go into the sublime feeling of the sameness of all things.

42.
The body and the world, filled with bliss

Contemplate that the whole world and your own body are simultaneously filled with bliss. Through the experience of your own nectar-like bliss, you will become one with the universal bliss.

—Verse 65

This sublime meditation goes directly to the heart of this path. In this tradition, our true nature is understood to be not just pure being and awareness but also an energetic throb of freedom and fullness that is often described as bliss. The Sanskrit term for this is *ananda*. Sometimes rendered as "joy" or "happiness" or "love," *ananda* has no precise English translation; there is no one word in English that captures the energetic fullness and multidimensional nature of the sublime experience of *ananda*.

Here, we dissolve the apparent separation of our personal self and the physical world by focusing on their common energetic reality— bliss. As in meditation 40, the idea of "simultaneous" tells us that this pervasion of bliss happens "all at once" and is not sequential.

Before embarking on the practice below, gather your energy so you have the strength to focus fully on the contemplation. When you're ready, begin the contemplation as best you can, and then let go into the experience.

This is one of the many meditations in this text that people with little or no background in meditation seem to intuitively grasp and experience with surprising ease.

~

Practice contemplating universal bliss

- Contemplate that the whole world and your own body are simultaneously filled with bliss. Stay with this.

- As the sublimely free energy of bliss begins to dissolve the boundaries of your individual self, let it carry you into the experience of universal bliss.

43.
Magic/delight

When watching magic performed, great bliss suddenly arises revealing the true nature of reality.

—Verse 66

When we see a magic trick—or anything else that catches us off guard in a magical way—in the moment of surprise our mind stops, and there is a flash of delight. We are in a state of mute wonder.

The same bliss of wonder, delight, and amazement is the focus of this meditation. We use our response to propel ourselves into a state beyond the mind, a state from where we spontaneously see the magical nature of life.

Our delight in what we are seeing, coupled with an amazed mind, become a doorway into an intuitive flash in which we remember that life is itself like a magic show, a dream—and not at all what our worried little self was thinking it to be!

This meditation encourages us to attend to the moments of surprise and delight that occur throughout our day.

The following contemplation can help prepare us to take full advantage of these moments.

~

Practice thinking of delight

- Bring to mind a memory of a time when you experienced surprise and delight.

- Focus on your reaction—feel fully your surprise and the wonderful sensation of your delight.

- In this thought-free moment, let the great bliss remind you of the true nature of reality.

- Remain alert for these moments as they occur throughout the day.

44.
The tingling ascent of energy

Close all the openings of the senses and focus on the awakened energy in the central channel slowly moving upward with the tickling sensation of an ant walking on your skin. This will lead to supreme bliss.

—Verse 67

The tickling of the tiny feet of an ant moving on our skin is a compelling sensation and can help us focus on the very subtle experience of the energy moving in the central channel. The focus on such a minute sensation, combined with the humor of such an utterly endearing example, helps carry us into the experience of bliss. Once again, the text has woven mundane life experience into a classical disciplined practice.

To help redirect our customarily outgoing energies, we are asked to close the openings of the senses, using the classical hand position introduced in meditation 13. In both these meditations, it can be effective to simply think of the hand position without doing it. In this meditation, we would then withdraw our attention from our senses and put our focus on the energy at the base of the spine.

~

Practice focusing on the spine

- Place the thumbs in the ears, the index fingers over the eyes, the middle fingers on the nostrils, the ring fingers above the lips, and the little fingers below the lips.

- Withdraw all energy from your senses, like a turtle pulling in its limbs.

- Focus your awareness at the base of your spine.

- Feel as though the great life energy is slowly moving up your spine with the tickling sensation of the tiny feet of an ant moving on your skin.

- Let this exquisite, heightened sensation of the central channel take you into bliss.

45.
Energy moving between the lower centers

Throw your mind, full of bliss, into the middle of the energy that moves from the second center down to the root and from the root center up to the second. Hold your attention here and experience the transcendent bliss of sexual union.

—Verse 68

A mind full of bliss is a wonderful thought!

Here, we throw that mind right into the middle of energy flowing up and down, between the center located at the base of the spine near the perineum and the center located near the spine at the level of the genitals. (Following the twelve-center system described in meditation 7, this the first and third chakras; following the more widely known seven-center system, this is the first and second chakras.) By focusing in meditation on the pulsing energy moving between these two centers, we can experience the bliss of sexual union and its transcendent energy.

~

Practice focusing on the first two centers

- Focus on the energy center located in the area of the perineum. Feeling or visualizing light or energy in this center can help activate the energetic sense of this center in your body. Then, either sense or visualize the second center a little distance above it.

- Now, feel the luminous awakened energy moving up and down between the two centers, from one center to the other. Stay with this energetic movement, up and down.

- As the energy builds in the space that exists between the two centers, these two currents—moving up and down—will begin to merge into each other, growing into an even stronger energy.

- When this happens, throw your mind, full of bliss, right into the middle of this extraordinary energy and let the experience take you into the universal bliss of sexual union—the great merge.

46.
Merge in the energy of orgasm

At the time of sexual union, the bliss experienced by absorption into the intensity at the end is the bliss of the transcendent. That same bliss is said to be your own true nature. Meditate on this bliss.

—Verse 69

The following six meditations, which are on embracing the senses and the natural pleasures of life, are some of the best known and loved meditations in this text. They are full of humanity and lack the judgmental voice that traditional spiritual texts take in approaching such subjects. Each of these meditations encourages us to focus on the moment of peak intensity in what is a natural experience—and then to use this heightened energy to move through the experience of pleasure into the bliss of pure being and oneness with all that is.

In this meditation on the energetic experience of lovemaking, rather than allowing the extraordinary energy of sexual orgasm to peak and dissipate, we are to shift our attention from the physical sensation to the energy of the intensity itself. As we become absorbed in the blissful intensity of this energy, our experience of separation begins to dissolve and we start to experience a transcendent bliss. At the moment of orgasm, instead of falling back into our familiar individual sense of self, we are to stay with the transcendent bliss, identifying with it, understanding that this bliss is our own true nature.

It is the last step—letting go of our original focus and allowing the energy to transport us into the highest dimensions of our self—that elevates what is a common, pleasurable experience to being a sublime and blissful meditative practice.

~

Practice merging with the energy of orgasm

- At the time of lovemaking, focus on the energy of this beautiful, sensual experience.

- As the energy reaches its peak of intensity, let go of any thoughts and merge completely into this blissful energy, allowing the intensity of the energy to carry you into your highest Self.

- Stay with the vibrating, pulsing, life-affirming energy. This highest and, supremely free bliss is your true nature.

47.
Memory of intensity leads to flood of delight

Even in the absence of a partner, the memory of the intensity of sexual bliss—the kissing and the touching—can bring a flood of bliss. Meditate on this bliss.

—Verse 70

In this meditation we focus on the flood of bliss that comes just from remembering the bliss of lovemaking. The practice is to remember a time of lovemaking and to stay with the details of this memory, lingering with the memories that have the strongest feeling and sense of aliveness to them.

We are to focus on the intensity of the aliveness in the memory, allowing the body to fully relive this energetic experience in the present moment. Once our memory has fully reawakened the wonderful intensity of the original experience, we are to let go of our memory of the events themselves and to shift our attention fully to the energy itself, understanding that this blissful energy is our true nature.

~

Practice merging with memory of touch

- Recall a deeply pleasurable memory of lovemaking. As much as you can, fully re-enter your memory of this act.

- Relive all the sensual aspects of the memory, allowing each of these to reawaken the wonderful way you and your body felt at the time.

- Once the intensity of the experience has become strong, let go of the details of the memory and focus instead on the flood of blissful energy itself. Stay with the breathtaking, vibrating, pulsing, throbbing, shimmering energy.

- Allow yourself to merge into this energy, knowing that this highest, supremely free bliss is your true nature.

48.
An instance of delight or love

At any time when great bliss arises, such as the joy of seeing a friend or relative after a long absence, meditate on the bliss itself, becoming one with it.

—Verse 71

Life is full of moments of happiness. The spontaneous arising of bliss at times such as these carries us beyond the boundaries of our mind. For a moment, we glimpse our true nature.

In this meditation, we focus on these moments of bliss. This can be done in the moment itself or later, by reliving our memory of a moment of happiness. The practice is simple. Once we become aware of the feeling of bliss coming up—either in the moment or in a memory—then we are to let go of the circumstance and to stay with the beauty of the feeling. We then allow the feeling to take us into the unconditional bliss of our true nature.

All of the meditations on sensory experience can be practiced either in the moment or through memory. The practice below makes use of memory. The advantage to exploring such experiences in this way is that it predisposes our mind to pay attention to them in the moments in which they arise.

Practice remembering a joyful sight

- Recall a time when you felt a joyous happiness, real bliss— such as when you saw an old friend after a long time.

- Focus on your feeling of bliss.

- Once the feeling is strong enough, let go of any thoughts about the circumstance or your friend.

- Focus on the profound happiness itself until you become it. This bliss is your true nature.

49.
The joy of taste

When you are filled with joy arising from the pleasure of eating and drinking, meditate on the fullness of this bliss and supreme bliss will arise.

—Verse 72

The pleasure of the sense of taste comes up so spontaneously. When we bite into something delicious, for a moment our mind stops and there is a flash of bliss. Also, most of us are familiar with the great pleasure of a good meal, particularly one eaten in good company.

We can extend these pleasant moments by pausing and lingering with the joy when it arises. As we learn how to stay with these moments of joy, they can take us into the great transcendent bliss.

Once again, the following practice employs a memory to help us be more alert to these moments when they happen spontaneously.

~

Practice remembering a delicious taste

- Remember a time when you tasted something delicious. Catch the moment of bliss and stay with it!

- Linger in the feeling, letting the feeling fill your whole body and heart and transport you into the experience of Oneness.

- Be alert for these moments of bliss as they occur throughout the day.

50.
The joy of song

When your mind is focused on the incomparable joy of music and other aesthetic delights, this joy is the same as the inner joy of a yogi who has transcended the mind through concentration. Become one with this happiness.

—Verse 73

These meditations on the senses are in themselves beautiful thoughts. Just the act of reading these meditations from time to time can take us into the sublime experience they describe.

In this tradition it is understood that the aesthetic beauty we perceive in our outer world is a reflection of the beauty within us. By remembering that the joy we experience in moments of aesthetic delight is the same as the joy we find in deep meditation, we engage outer beauty, which can be fleeting, to remind ourselves of the inner joy that is always present when we go beyond the mind.

~

Practice focusing on aesthetic delight

- Focus on the pleasure you feel when you hear music that transports you—or when you experience any other moment of aesthetic delight such as seeing something beautiful or smelling an exquisite fragrance.

- Let the energy of this aesthetic beauty transport you into a thought-free state where you become one with the sublime blissful experience.

51.
Wherever the mind finds satisfaction leads to bliss

Wherever your mind finds satisfaction, focus it there, and the essence of your deepest happiness will manifest.

—Verse 74

The Sanskrit word for "satisfaction" is *tushti*, which has many subtle, aesthetic resonances. Generally, the word implies a disarmingly simple and peaceful sense of fullness. What this meditation points out is that a feeling of satisfaction is an extraordinarily beautiful doorway into its source, the fullness of unconditional bliss. In other words, when we focus on satisfaction, we can experience the much deeper bliss of pure being that lies just underneath.

As with the previous meditations on the senses, once again we are to look at the events in our life. In this meditation, we are to notice any moment of satisfaction where our mind comes to rest for a moment, where it is content to relax into the pleasurable fullness of this experience. The sense of satisfaction could come up at the end of a fulfilling experience, such as having spent time with close friends or after completing a challenging task. Or it could come at times of beauty, or love, or happiness, or pleasure.

The idea is to look for these moments in our life and to stay with the experience, with the feeling of satisfaction, and allow the feeling to take us into the fullness of being. Again, thinking deeply about this teaching predisposes our mind to spontaneously finding these moments in life.

The following is an example of using memory.

~

Practice remembering moments of satisfaction

- Let yourself recall various moments of satisfaction.
- Linger with these memories. Feel how they can be a doorway into a much deeper and fuller experience of peaceful happiness.
- Stay with this feeling and let it take you into the sublime.

52.
The threshold before sleep

Concentrate on the state just before you fall asleep but after your awareness of the external world has fallen away. Enter into this threshold state—between waking and sleep—which is illuminated by the great energy of Consciousness.

—Verse 75

Another way of stepping outside of the habitual flow of our consciousness is to catch the moment when we are about to fall asleep. Our mind is no longer in its familiar waking state and hasn't yet entered into its sleep state. Here, in this liminal space between the two familiar states, we can glimpse the immensity of the awareness that is always in the background of our changing mental states. As we catch this moment and enter into it, we enter the original, pristine, unconditioned vastness of our awareness and its spectacularly free energy.

As with many of these exercises, it is helpful to contemplate this experience ahead of time. We can use a memory of this experience to help us isolate and more keenly feel the exact moment we fall away from the waking state. We have made this shift thousands of times. It was just never pointed out to us that we could actually witness the experience. The very act of observing our mind begin to shift states is, in itself, exhilarating. We can do this witnessing only from the part of our awareness that is not lost in the experience, and this aspect of ourselves is by its very nature already free.

From this perspective, we can then enter into the gap between states and return to the vastness of awareness and the extraordinary energy and immensity of our true nature.

~

Practice as you fall asleep

- Let yourself observe the moment of falling asleep. Feel your way into the experience, slowing everything down so you can catch the exact moment you leave the waking state and its thoughts but haven't yet entered the sleep state.

- This is a very alert state. You are momentarily experiencing the aspect of your consciousness that is the observing awareness and is always there in the background. Suddenly, it is in the foreground.

- This aspect of you is utterly free. Stay with it and enter fully into the immensity of your Consciousness.

53.
Luminous space

Steadily gaze at a space filled with the variegated shafts of light from the sun or a lamp. Your very essence, too, will be illuminated.

—Verse 76

Incense smoke rising gently through rays of light, specks of dust in the air floating in light beams, shafts of light breaking through clouds, rainbows, moonlight...In all these scenes, light beams make the space they travel through luminous. The ethereal beauty of these transitory and magical moments reminds us of the beauty that is within.

~

Practice focusing on the play of light

- Notice a moment when the exquisite play of light catches your attention: incense smoke rising gently through shafts of light, specks of dust in the air floating through light beams...

- Enter into the space of the light itself, allowing yourself to merge with the sublime beauty that is the very nature of your true Self.

54.
Classical hand gestures

While practicing the classical postures known as *karakini,*
krodhana, bhairavi, lelihana, and *khechari,* be ready for the flash
of intuitive wisdom in which the highest Truth is illuminated.

—Verse 77

These classical postures are known as *mudras,* a term that refers
to any posture of the body or mind that is used to enhance our
focus in meditation. The five *mudras* named in this meditation are
highly esoteric and involve disciplined dispositions of the body
and mind. Each of these postures engages a different aspect of our
consciousness.

The key to each of the practices below is to be receptive to an
intuitive flash of the Truth as it appears.

~

Practice being a skeleton

Karakini means "skeleton." In this meditation, you imagine yourself sitting as a skeleton, which is meant to help induce a feeling of detachment.

- Sit quietly and imagine yourself as nothing but a skeleton. Let yourself feel what it would be like to be long dead and nothing but bones.
- Feel the state of detachment that comes as you realize the impermanence of life.
- Stay with this until there is an intuitive flash of the great timeless truth of life and the unchanging presence of your being.

~

Practice being angry

Krodhana literally means "anger" and refers to a tensing of the entire body as a prelude to tranquility.

- Sit quietly and begin to tense your entire body as if in a rage.
- Let the intensity build, right from the toes, through all the limbs and face.
- Once the rage has reached its peak, suddenly release it entirely.
- Notice the feeling of tranquility, and rest in it.

~

Practice becoming aware of being

Bhairavi is the feminine form of Bhairava and is a name of the great creative energy of Consciousness. The posture in this *mudra* is a mental one in which the non-conceptual awareness of both your interior world and the outer world are held simultaneously.

- Sit quietly and become deeply aware of your own being.
- While holding this inner awareness, simultaneously expand your awareness around yourself in all directions.
- Allow your awareness to be both deeply interior and simultaneously spread out into the world all around you.

~

Practice seeing yourself as light

Lelihana means "flame" and refers to the practice of seeing your consciousness as an extension of the light of universal Consciousness.

- Sit quietly and contemplate yourself as a luminous field of energy within a much vaster field of energy.
- Feel the light of your consciousness as an extension of and, at the same time, one with the universal light of Consciousness.

~

Practice curling back your tongue

Khechari refers to the practice of curling the tip of the tongue to the roof of the mouth (or back of the nasal passages) while focusing intently on the center between the eyebrows. The intense focus of energy in these regions of the head can propel you into the state beyond the mind.

- Sitting quietly, keep the tip of your tongue curled to the back of the roof of your mouth while focusing intently on the center between the eyebrows.

- Let the energy build and carry you into the state beyond all thought.

55.
Sitting relaxed on one buttock

Sitting on a soft seat, balance all your weight on just one buttock. Keeping your arms and legs relaxed without support, your mind will become transcendent.

—Verse 78

Shifting our center of balance out of its familiar position and over to one side engages a unique level of interior focus. Holding this focus has the spontaneous effect of stopping our thoughts. The combination of our steady attention to balance and its natural inhibition of our thinking precipitates a gentle yet clear shift into the thought-free state.

Notice the humor and play in following the most complex and esoteric meditation instructions in the text with an instruction that is utterly delightful. Although the text maintains great respect for each of the traditions from which it draws, it rarely passes up an opportunity to point out how immediate the shift of attention from our conceptual self to essence can be.

This meditation playfully bypasses all ideas of serious yogic effort with this simple, childlike exploration.

~

Practice sitting on one buttock

- Sitting comfortably, shift all your weight over to one buttock. Keep the rest of your body relaxed with a floating feeling.

- Notice how your focus on this unique shift in balance naturally stills your mind.

- Let go into the thought-free state.

56.
The space between the arms

Sitting comfortably, form your arms into a circle and gaze into the space enclosed by them. Through this absorption, the mind becomes peaceful.

—Verse 79

The circle, which has no beginning and no end, is a universal symbol of infinity. Forming a circle with your arms and gazing into the gentle embrace of emptiness, the mind becomes deeply peaceful.

The arms can be placed out in front of the body or over the head. Each position has its own effect.

~

Practice gazing at the space between your arms

- Form a circle with your arms.
- Gaze into the space contained by the circle.
- Let the gentle embrace of the emptiness take your mind into a deeply peaceful state.

57.
A fixed gaze on an object, without thoughts

Steadily gaze at an object without the support of any thoughts about it. You will very quickly be in the state beyond all thought.

—Verse 80

Usually, when we look at something, our mind simultaneously has many thoughts about it, rather than our just seeing the object directly as it is. Gazing at something without allowing any internal dialogue pulls us out of our habituated mental chatter and into the felt experience of the vivid, brilliant present.

This practice is extremely accessible. All it requires is a clear intention to pull our attention away from thinking and give ourselves wholly to gazing at the object.

~

Practice gazing at anything

- Choose any object in your field of vision. Gaze at it steadily with the firm intention to see it directly without any thoughts about it.

- With all your awareness focused on your direct experience of the object without any thoughts about it, notice that you enter the vivid aliveness of the present moment.

- Without any thoughts about it, you become one with the object.

58.
Soundless *ha*

Keep your tongue in the middle of your open mouth and fix your attention in the center of the open space. Repeat the sound *ha* silently in your mind and dissolve into tranquility.

—Verse 81

This delightful meditation on the space inside our open mouth once again focuses on the quality of space as a natural way of entering the non-dual state. In this meditation, we place the tongue in the middle of the space of our open mouth—or we can curl the tongue up and back with the tip inserted into the cavity of the cranium at the back of the roof of the mouth (as we did in meditation 54 with *khechari mudra*). Either of these tongue positions adds extra sensation in the area to help with the focus of our energy and attention.

Once the position of the tongue is established, we're to repeat the syllable *ha* silently in our mind. The syllable *ha* is symbolic of the great creative energy. Repeating *ha* silently in our mind pulls our awareness to the syllable's energetic, pulsing source. Approaching the source energy, our mind dissolves, and we enter into a sublime tranquility.

~

Practice saying a silent *ha*

- Hold your mouth open and place your tongue so that its tip is in the middle of the open space. Let the position of the tip of your tongue help you focus in the middle of the space of your open mouth.

- As your mind begins to relax into the sensation of this space, repeat the sound *ha* silently in your mind.

- Let the gentle burst of energy that comes help to carry you beyond all thought and into the peaceful tranquility of pure being.

59.
Body without support

While either sitting or lying down, contemplate that your body is without any support, as if suspended in space. As your mind, too, becomes supportless, it is freed of thoughts, and you cease being a reservoir of old mental dispositions.

—Verse 82

Our conventional, limited self reflexively uses thoughts to orient itself in life. In heightening our awareness of how we lean on our thoughts for support, we give ourselves the choice not to go there and to stay instead in the thought-free state of pure awareness. This awareness is our true nature that exists prior to thought. In the true Self, we cease being a reservoir of old stories!

A lovely, simple meditation.

~

Practice focusing on the sense of your body floating

- While sitting or lying down, concentrate on the feeling of your body gently floating without any support, as if floating on a cloud or in space.

- Let the comfortable relaxed feeling of your body help your mind to let go of whatever it usually clings to.

- Let yourself merge into the profoundly peaceful feeling of the state beyond all thought.

60.
Swaying

Dear One, when swaying as you might when in a moving vehicle or when just sitting and swaying by yourself, focus on the slow rocking motion of your body. In the peaceful state of mind that follows, you enter into the stream of divine Consciousness.

—Verse 83

As with the previous meditation, this practice is exquisitely simple and extraordinarily effective. Many people who say they can't meditate find themselves almost immediately going into a wonderful state when they follow these instructions.

In this meditation we are to focus on—or just to remember—natural moments of movement and swaying, like the swaying motion of an old train or the gentle rocking of a boat out on a lake. We instinctively rock babies to calm them. This gentle rocking is soothing to the body.

As we consciously focus on this swaying motion, our mind merges into the sensation and naturally calms. In that tranquil state we can begin to feel the stream of divine Consciousness.

~

Practice merging into swaying

- Recall a time when your body was swaying, or just sit quietly and begin to gently sway.

- Focus on this slow rocking motion.

- Let your mind merge into the calming flow of the gentle movement, and float into the exquisite stream of divine Consciousness.

61.
Open sky

With steady awareness, gaze continuously at a cloudless sky. You will enter infinity at once.

—Verse 84

Spaciousness is one of the most easily accessed qualities of our awareness. The open space of a clear sky is an ancient symbol of the Infinite. By steadily gazing at a clear sky, our mind opens into the peaceful vastness and for a moment we touch infinity. It is the clarity of our intention that turns the sky into a luminous doorway.

With this meditation, as with many, thinking about it beforehand seeds the idea in our mind and makes it easier for us to remember to do it in the moment an opportunity arises.

~

Practice focusing on the open sky

- Remember an experience of the open sky, or look up at the sky.
- Gaze steadily at the vast expanse until you feel your mind starting to merge with it.
- Become one with the boundless space and touch infinity.

62.
Open space in the head

Contemplate a vast sky, which is the very form of the Infinite, as if it were completely within your head. You will enter the luminous state.

—Verse 85

In the previous meditation, we let our mind merge outward into the open space of the sky. In this meditation, we imagine the entire sky inside our own head. The vast spaciousness is now interior.

With thoughts far away, we enter a luminous state.

~

Practice putting the sky inside your head

- Sit quietly and imagine a vast clear sky as being completely within your head.

- Stay with the extraordinary feeling of immensity inside of you.

- Rest in the spacious, thought-free experience and the accompanying luminous state.

63.
All states are only Consciousness

Contemplate that the three states—waking (where there is a limited type of knowledge that produces the sense of duality) dreaming (which is filled with impressions of the outer world), and deep sleep (which is filled with darkness)—are just different forms of Consciousness. Realizing this, you are filled with the splendor of the Infinite.

—Verse 86

At the time these meditations were written, the mind was commonly understood to have three states—waking, dreaming, and deep sleep. We all move through the three states every twenty-four hours. What this meditation is pointing out is that in each of these states we experience a completely different reality.

The waking state is dominated by the intensity of our sense perceptions and our feeling of being a unique individual in the midst of a vast field of physical objects, other people, and events.

In the dream state, our attention shifts away from the physical and anchors itself in dream world where our thoughts, images, and feelings can seem just as tangible to us as the material reality of our waking state. Only our dreams are not real in the same way. Our dreams are made wholly of mental energy.

In deep sleep, we enter a state where there are no longer even images of physical reality or of our corresponding sense of ourselves as an individual. We experience only the vast darkness of the deep sleep dimension of our consciousness.

Contemplating that all three states are just various forms of the same Consciousness pushes us into the witness state from which we view all three states. This is the awareness that is always present, in the background of our experience. From this vantage point, we can observe each dimension of our experience. The immensity of the witness state fills us with amazement and delight.

~

Practice contemplating all states as Consciousness

- Contemplate that the three states of waking, dreaming, and deep sleep are just different forms of the same Consciousness.

- As you begin to see this, rest in the immensity and amazement of what you are experiencing.

64.
The dark of night

If you long to experience the great mystery, contemplate the magnitude of the darkness of a dark night in the darkest phase of the moon's cycle.

—Verse 87

The awe inspired by the sheer magnitude of a dark night sky is a powerful entryway into the mystical. The vast blackness of the night sky has stirred awe in many a soul throughout time.

In this third meditation on the sky, the focus is on the magnitude of the intense darkness of the night sky and the overwhelming awe that this stirs in us. We contemplate the night sky's immensity until we feel ourselves touching the great mystery.

This practice is most powerful when done on a moonless night, far away from city lights.

~

Practice looking at a night sky

- Gaze up at a dark night sky and contemplate the sheer magnitude of the darkness.

- Stay with the immensity of the experience.

- Feel yourself touching the great mystery.

65.
The dark of night: eyes closed and open

In the same way, meditate with your eyes closed on the profound darkness of night spreading out within you until you become one with the Infinite.

—Verse 88

Contemplating the dark night sky within ourselves is a powerful way of entering the causal level of our consciousness, which can appear as a pure velvet blackness. Because we are entering the darkness fully aware, instead of falling asleep into it as we usually do, we become the witness of it.

From the perspective of the witness, we can take in the enormous power of this causal level. The experience of pure being becomes quite vivid.

~

Practice seeing the night sky inside you

- Recall an experience of a dark night sky. Meditate on the darkness spreading inside of you until you become one with the Infinite.

66.
The restraint of one sense

When one of the sense organs is obstructed in its function, either naturally or intentionally, the mind becomes introverted. Focus on the emptiness of that sense that transcends all difference and become one with the Self of all.

—Verse 89

The yogis used to practice *pratyahara,* the total withdrawal of all attention from their senses, as a preliminary step toward *samadhi,* the complete stilling of their minds. Sometimes yogis would block the openings of the senses in the head with their hands to help inhibit the outflowing attention as we did in meditations 13 and 44. In this meditation, we are focusing on the experience when just one sense is blocked.

To get a feeling for this, purposefully heighten your experience of what you can hear. Then, plug your ears with your thumbs. This action blocks external sounds and heightens your experience of the emptiness, which itself is a gateway into unity. This blocking off is most easily accomplished with sight or sound, although you can be creative and find ways to do this with any of the other senses.

Notice that the text is once again taking a practice that could seem intense and austere, and pointing out that it already happens naturally in our lives. This happens, for example, when the lights go out in a room and you can't see or when you are under water and all surface sounds disappear.

The text instructs us to notice these moments when they happen, to enjoy the natural introversion of our mind, to stay with the exquisite subtle sense of emptiness, and to let this experience take us into the state where there is no separation.

The following is a practice that blocks the sense of hearing.

~

Practice restraining hearing

- Focus on your sense of hearing, and then purposely inhibit your hearing by placing your thumbs in your ears.

- Concentrate on the lack of external sound.

- Stay with the exquisite, subtle sense of emptiness, and let this take you into infinity.

67.
Saying the letter *a*

Beloved, recite the letter *a* aloud, without the company of any other letters. A great torrent of divine wisdom will immediately appear.

—Verse 90

A is the first letter of the Sanskrit alphabet and represents the first principle of creation. It is considered to be the highest Reality in the form of sound and appears frequently in the key words of many sacred traditions: Allah, alleluia, shalom, Rama…

Repeating the sacred letter *a* without any other letters accompanying it is symbolic of the highest principle in itself, utterly free of any levels of manifestation. This is the creative principle vibrating in its own transcendence before assuming any form.

When we're aware of the sublime meaning this letter embodies before we pronounce it, then this very knowledge orients our mind to the unified field of pure awareness from which the sound appears and into which it once again merges.

The suggestive metaphor of being flooded by a torrent of divine wisdom beautifully embodies this text's emphasis of the energetic aspect of reality.

~

Practice saying the letter *a*

- Take a moment to gather your attention and energy.
- When you're ready, say aloud the letter *a*.
- Hold steady in the torrent of divine wisdom that appears in this timeless moment.

68.
Ha!

Fix your mind without any support on the end of the short sound *ha*, and you will touch the eternal.

—Verse 91

The sound *ha* is an aspirated form of the primal letter *a* and represents the great creative energy of Consciousness. As in the previous meditation, we use sound itself to help us shift states. In this meditation, it is a sound that honors the feminine aspect of the highest.

We gather our full intention and energy, and then, in one short, loud burst, we throw our mind into the space at the end of the sound, allowing the burst of energy to catapult us out of our thoughts and into timeless presence.

~

Practice saying *ha!*

- Gather your energy, and then in one short, loud burst, say *ha*.

- Focus intently on the end of the sound.

- Let the burst of energy catapult you out of thinking.

- Remain completely still as your mind touches the Eternal.

69.
Vast as the sky

Meditate on yourself as a vast sky, unlimited in all directions. Freed of all thoughts, the energy that has become your mind will return to its true form.

—Verse 92

In this much-loved meditation, we consciously identify with the sky, vast and unlimited in all directions, until we return to the boundless free nature of our true Self.

Our mind is nothing but a condensed form of the great universal Consciousness.

When we meditate on ourselves as a vast sky, unlimited in all directions, this focus helps the mind to release its limiting grip and return to its source—the vast, boundless freedom of pure Consciousness, our own timeless being that has always been there.

Notice that there are subtle variations on space in many of these meditations. In meditation 61, the focus is on our experience of outer space. In meditation 62, the focus on our experience of inner space. Here, we are to focus on our own self as the very form of spaciousness.

~

Practice meditating on yourself as a vast sky

- Meditate on yourself as a vast sky, unlimited in all directions.
- Hold steady with this thought and the felt sense of your awareness, extending out around you infinitely in all directions. This is your true Self.

70.
The sharp point of intensity

Piercing one of your limbs with a sharp, pointed object like a needle and focusing your consciousness at that exact point of intensity, you will approach the fresh, clear nature of pure Consciousness.

—Verse 93

In this meditation we use the intensity of pain as the entryway into the experience of the Self. Pressing a sharp object like a pin against our skin creates a vivid and intense sensation. The energy that lies at the core of any sensation is nothing but the great universal Consciousness in that form. The idea in this meditation is to focus on the energy of the sensation rather than any thoughts we may have about it.

We enter into this point of intensity, penetrating through what we would usually label as pain, seeing it, feeling it for what it actually is: pure energy. By staying with the experience as merely energy, we enter the experience of the great universal life force.

Please note that there is no need to puncture your skin in this meditation. It works just as well when you use the pin or needle to press the skin gently.

~

Practice on a point of intensity

- Gently press a sharp object like a pin or a needle against your skin.

- Focus on the point of intensity. Stay with just the sensation, rather than indulging in any thoughts about it.

- Don't resist the sensation. Instead, be curious about it. Keep penetrating into the sensation itself with your awareness until you see and feel the sensation as nothing but energy.

- Stay with this energy and let it take you into the experience of pure Consciousness.

71.
No mind

Contemplate firmly, "I have no mind." Without thoughts, you are free!

—Verse 94

In this meditation, we use the mind to short-circuit the mind! The very thought of having no mind causes the mind to try to form an image of what this means. In the process, the mind is catapulted beyond its familiar self and into the thought-free state. If we are alert to this moment and stay with it, we find ourselves sublimely free of all thoughts.

In a very Zen-like manner, this meditation points out that by just negating the mind, all thoughts of separation are transcended. And there we are, in thought-free Oneness, the famous Zen "no mind" state!

There are two classical approaches to the experience of Oneness. The first of these is to negate the experience of everything that appears as separate by contemplating ideas such as *I am not my body, I am not my emotions, I am not my thoughts,* until all that is left for us to identify with is the one that is aware of all this—the pure awareness that is the core of our being.

The second approach to Oneness is to embrace everything that appears as separate from us. We contemplate, *I am one with every- thing that exists.* As we have seen, this text employs both approaches.

This meditation is, of course, an example of the first of these. They are both examples of creative identification—*bhava,* in Sanskrit— wherein we experiment with perceiving and experiencing through a specific inspired thought or feeling that reflects our true Self.

~

Practice the no-mind meditation

- Repeat to yourself, "I have no mind."
- Notice the thought-free state.
- Stay there.

72.
Contemplate the function of the five powers of limitation

The universal creative power deludes us and resides in the five powers of limitation such as the power of restricted activity. Contemplate the functions of the various principles in the creation process in this way and you will no longer remain separate.

—Verse 95

Don't skip over this meditation because it sounds complicated. It is one of the most intelligent and powerful contemplations in this text!

In order to have experiences as a human being, one of the things Consciousness does is to focus itself into unique points of awareness in the time/space dimension. This is how we can have the human experience of being a unique individual. Consciousness does this by limiting its powers at the highest levels, where we are one with all activity, all knowledge, all desire, all time, and all places.

The universal creative power—known in Sanskrit by the term *maya*—limits our infinite sense of being in five specific ways:

1. action—our experience of being able to do anything is limited to just the actions of our individual experience.

2. knowledge—our sense of knowing everything is limited to knowledge of only certain particulars.

3. will—our love of experiencing everything is limited to wanting only certain things.

4. time—our sense of eternity is limited to a specific time.

5. space—our experience of universal presence is limited to a particular place.

When we become aware of these limiting forces, they start to lose their binding effect on us.

Although these concepts may seem challenging on first reading, they are not as abstract as they might appear. In working with the practice below, many people are surprised at how easily they can grasp intuitively what is being said and suddenly find themselves propelled into a unified state of Consciousness.

⁓

Practice contemplating the five limitations

· Begin by settling into a sense of relaxed, open awareness.

· One by one, contemplate each of the five experiences of limitation—limited action, limited knowledge, limited will, limited time, and limited space.

· Let yourself begin to see and feel how each limitation happens at subtle levels in your consciousness.

· Once you actually see how each limitation happens, notice the limitations start to lose their binding power. You become free of them. Your sense of separation from the universe dissolves and you return to your true nature.

73.
Find the source of desire

Observe a flash of desire at the moment it springs up. Put an end to it, and there alone become absorbed.

—Verse 96

This meditation focuses on where we place our attention. Usually, we notice only the object of our desires—the Twinkie, sleep, a relationship, world domination...Particularly strong desires can seem almost solid, as if they are a thing that has a grip on us. But when we move our attention from the content of a desire to the energy behind the surface appearance of this desire, its seeming hypnotic grip dissolves, and we begin to feel the much freer life-energy that is just underneath the desire—that is its source.

The Sanskrit term *shaman*, which appears in this meditation, literally means "tranquility" and "an absence of passion." The word is more usually translated as "mental discipline" or "self-control." Choosing to be tranquil in response to a desire is a subtle way of inhibiting the desire from taking form. You might experiment with this response and see if it helps you release the grip of a desire.

This meditation can be done using a memory as well as catching a desire as it occurs in real time. In the following practice, we work with a memory.

~

Practice looking at desire

- Remember a strong desire.
- Give your attention to the initial flash or pulse of this desire.
- Stay with this initial burst of energy, before it turns into thoughts and images.
- Feel the energy itself, free of content—throbbing, pulsing, shimmering, surging, flashing.
- Stay with the feeling and follow it back to where it comes from—the great unified field of infinite potential.

74.
Who am I?

"Before desire and knowledge arise in me, who am I? I am That."
Become absorbed in and identified with this understanding
until you are one with it.

—Verse 97

"Who am I—what am I—before I have a desire or thought?" This
powerful question redirects our attention to the unconditioned
awareness from which all our thoughts and desires appear and into
which they disappear.

In this meditation, rather than trying to find this unconditioned
awareness by inhibiting a specific thought or desire, we move our
attention to the pure awareness that existed before we got lost in our
thoughts or desires. This pure awareness that is prior to our thoughts
is our true nature. It is utterly free of any limited identification.
Know this to be your real Self. Stay in it; become absorbed in it;
identify with it until you and this pure awareness are one.

~

Practice looking past desire and thought

- Ask yourself the question, "Before desire and knowledge arise in me, who am I?"

- Become still and follow your thoughts and desires back to where they come from. Stay there.

- Become absorbed in this space of pure awareness and potential that exists prior to your thoughts and desires.

- This is you at an undifferentiated level, before you have become anything. This is your true nature—completely free, unbounded Consciousness.

- Let go into pure Consciousness. Identify with it. Be it.

75.
The moment of desire or knowledge

When a desire or knowledge arises, focus intently on the understanding that it is nothing but your own consciousness, and you will then realize the essence of all creative principles.

—Verse 98

Just as the one Consciousness creates universe after universe out of itself, we too create endless desires and thoughts out of our own consciousness. Our desires and thoughts are nothing but our own utterly free and creative conscious energy, spontaneously appearing in those forms.

If we forget this basic truth, our desires and thoughts seem to have an independent existence. Not realizing them to be our own consciousness that appears for a moment in this form, we react to these thoughts as if they were a concrete reality—materially true and with an existence separate from ourselves.

Fascination with our desires and thoughts can keep us on the surface of our awareness—and cause us to miss the greater, foundational part of ourselves. In this meditation, instead of trying to stop or control desires and thoughts, we are to bear in mind that all that exists is only a temporary appearance of Consciousness. This means that our desires and thoughts are, likewise, nothing but pure conscious energy taking this particular form for a moment. We can use this understanding to break the hypnotic trance that has us looking at our desires and thoughts as if they had solidity and an independent reality.

Once we remember that these are only the one Consciousness appearing in that form for a moment, our attention is no longer trapped in the content of the desire or thought. Our fascination now shifts to the seemingly magical arising and subsiding of patterns of thought and desire within the greater field of universal energy, which is nothing but our very own Self.

~

Practice focusing on desires and thoughts as consciousness

- Focus intently on the understanding that your desires and thoughts are nothing but your own consciousness in that form for a moment.

- As the hypnotic grip of your thoughts and desires relaxes, notice the open free space of your consciousness.

- Stay with the pulsing energy of your consciousness and the inner knowing—that this is how worlds are created.

76.
All knowledge is without cause

From the perspective of the highest Reality, all knowledge is baseless, deceptive, and without cause. It doesn't belong to anybody. Contemplate this and become free.

—Verse 99

This meditation honors those spiritual traditions that see life as a dream or an illusion. From the perspective of the field of pure energy potential that creates an infinite number of realities, our little mental formulations about the immensity are like tiny fruit flies buzzing for a moment in a shaft of sunlight. They are incapable of even beginning to describe the totality. If we keep thinking them, we stay trapped within their tiny sphere of mental formulation. They may be useful for describing things at many levels of reality, but they can't describe the field of infinite potential itself. This is beyond words.

The practice of consciously questioning the validity of our thoughts—of *any* thought—and of recognizing the inherent limitation of *all* thought with regard to the bigger picture is a powerful way of shifting our attention into the thought-free state.

This meditation frees us from the trap of our thoughts by pointing out that from the awakened perspective, all thoughts are inherently limiting and deceptive. No thought can capture the extraordinary, multidimensional nature of our experience. Even ideas about the highest Truth are just that—ideas about the highest Truth and not the experience of Reality!

Ideas can point toward the Truth, but at some point, we will need to leave them behind and enter directly into the experience.

The famous Zen saying, "The finger pointing at the moon is not the moon," captures this understanding beautifully.

As we begin to see the inherently limiting nature of our thoughts, we can catch glimpses of a much greater reality in which our thoughts appear and disappear. Released from the prison of our opinions and limited perceptions, we are now free to let go and enter the thought-free experience of Oneness.

~

Practice seeing knowledge as baseless

- Tell yourself that from the perspective of the highest Reality, all knowledge is baseless, deceptive, and without cause. It doesn't belong to anybody.

- Contemplate this and become free.

77.
Consciousness is the same in all bodies

Contemplate that the same Consciousness is present in every form; there is no difference in it anywhere. Realizing that everything is pervaded by this Consciousness, you transcend the boundaries of personal, separate experience, triumphantly rising above transmigratory existence.

—Verse 100

This powerful contemplation affirms the sublime oneness of all things.

In this tradition, it is understood that everything that exists is nothing but a momentary appearance of a universal energy within the field of time and space. There is only one substance appearing as everything in the universe. When we hold to this thought, we begin to break through the surface appearance of physical solidity and the separate existence of things. As we hold our mind accountable for seeing the underlying Oneness in each person, animal, tree, situation, thought…then the illusion of separation begins to dissolve. We glimpse the Oneness.

In the blissful recognition of the underlying unity of all life, we transcend the boundaries of our personal existence.

~

Practice contemplating that all is one Consciousness

- Contemplate that the same one Consciousness is present in all forms—all people, all things, all situations, all universes, all dimensions. There is no difference in the basic substratum of anything, anywhere.

- Everything that exists is nothing but a momentary appearance of the universal energy within the field of time and space.

- Realize this and transcend the boundaries of your separate existence.

78.
Holding steady with an intense emotion

When in the various states of craving, anger, greed, delusion, arrogance, or envy, steady your mind, and the reality which underlies these states will alone remain.

—Verse 101

The intensity of negative emotions can be a powerful springboard into the experience of unity. The practice in this meditation is to steady our mind so firmly in the heat of the moment, that the mind is immobilized along with the rampant thoughts that usually accompany such emotion.

Without these attendant thoughts, the emotion is now just intense energy in our body. Freed of its surface appearance, the emotion can appear to us as it truly is: pure, intense aliveness. When we stay fully present with intense energy—without thinking about it—its very intensity powerfully heightens our awareness. In the freedom of this vividly alive presence, we can remember the Oneness, the love, that lies beneath all the appearances of life.

Contemplating this ahead of time will help make it easier to do in the passion of the moment.

~

Practice thinking of an intense and difficult moment

- Remember a moment of an intense, difficult emotion.

- Relive this moment; this time see yourself firmly steadying your mind and stopping all thoughts about what is happening.

- Notice that without these thoughts, the emotion is nothing more than intense energy in your body.

- If you don't let the energy go into thought, notice that the energy itself naturally heightens your experience of being present.

- Rather than being trapped in your old response, you now have the possibility of infinite other ways of responding.

- From this perspective, you can see through the surface of life to the underlying Oneness of all things. Stay here.

79.
The illusory nature of the cosmos

Meditate on the universe as a magic show, or as a painting, or as a passing phenomenon. Contemplating the illusory nature of everything in this way, great happiness arises.

—Verse 102

Contemplating that our life is like a magic show, or a painting, or just a passing event can help to disentangle us from our usual thoughts about what happens. We begin to perceive the dreamlike nature of life—a thrilling and liberating idea to consider!

Many of the great wisdom traditions tell us that life is a dream. People from all cultures have reported intuitive glimpses of this understanding. Meditating on life as a dream, or as a magic show, or as a painting, or as a passing phenomenon shifts us into the position of a witness, a state from where we can appreciate the illusory nature of life.

When we remember this, our sense of separation falls away and, as the verse says, great happiness arises.

~

Practice seeing the universe as a dream

- Contemplate the passing, magical, dreamlike nature of the universe. Bring to mind any memories of this that you might have had at different times in your life.

- Entertain the thought that life is like a magic show, or a painting, or a passing phenomenon and let these images help you remember the dreamlike quality of life and the great happiness that comes with remembering this truth.

80.
Beyond pain and pleasure

Dear Friend, don't let your mind dwell on either pain or pleasure. Get to know the essence of the middle state.

—Verse 103

In the ground between any two emotional states lies the middle state, our center, our true Self. From here, we can feel the polarities of life but remain unaffected by them. When we dwell on either pain or pleasure, this traps our attention in just one aspect of life and pulls us out of our true nature—the free and loving witness of the flow of life.

In this meditation, we are to contemplate what it would be like to hold steady in our center rather than to dwell on either pain or pleasure. By repeatedly thinking this over, we begin to experience the unshakable essence of our true Self.

This and the two meditations that follow are all contemplations—that is, something to think about—and practices, something to do.

~

Practice not dwelling on pain or pleasure

- Think deeply about what it would feel like to not dwell on pain or pleasure but, rather, to hold steady in your center. Imagine yourself in the future, experiencing pain or pleasure.

- See yourself, as you go through the experience, remaining in your center.

- Let the intuitive knowledge, the feeling of how to stay centered in the midst of pain or pleasure, awaken in you.

- Feel how, from your center, when these life experiences occur, you can have the deep pleasure of meeting them from your true Self.

81.
"I am everywhere!"

Abandoning all attachment to your body, contemplate "I am everywhere." With your mind firmly determined not to see another, you will become happy.

—Verse 104

There are two steps to this contemplation. First, let go of all thoughts of yourself as a separate entity and rest in what is left—your sense of pure being, the pure *I am*. Second, with a mind determined not to see anything as separate from yourself, assert, "I am everywhere; all this is me." In this way extending your sense of *I am* out into all beings, all times, and all places, your sense of separation dissolves. You begin to experience profound happiness.

~

Practice resting in the pure "I am"

- Let go of all thoughts of yourself as a separate body and rest in what is left—your sense of simple being, the pure I am.

- Now, with a mind determined not to see anything as separate from yourself, assert, "I am everywhere; I am in all things."

- Expand your sense of "I am" to all beings and places and times.

- As your sense of separation dissolves, rest in the sublime happiness that arises.

82.
Knowledge and desire are common to all

Contemplate "Knowledge and desire appear not only within me; they are common to all things, even objects like a jar!" You will become all-pervasive.

—Verse 105

The whole universe is just one appearance of the unified field of infinite potential. The universe we know is Consciousness, vibrating in very specific patterns, including the time/space continuum. The information in this energy that causes it to vibrate in a unique pattern is known as its "knowledge." The extraordinary impulse to move from the subtle level of potential into the physical dimension is known as its "desire." In this way, knowledge and desire are common to everything in the universe.

Usually, we wouldn't think that we have anything in common with a jar. But each atom in the jar is alive and vibrates in a specific pattern. And, as we've just explored, that unique pattern is its knowledge and its appearance in this dimension is its desire to be. In this way, the jar is like us!

When we contemplate that knowledge and desire appear not only in ourselves but are common to everything in the universe, our sense of isolation falls away and we feel a profound camaraderie with all that is.

~

Practice feeling knowledge and desire in all things

- Contemplate the statement "Knowledge and desire appear not only within me; they are common to all things, even objects like a jar!"

- Feel how at a deep level, you have these qualities in common with everything in the universe.

- As your sense of being a separate self falls away, let go into the feeling of being one with all.

83.
The subject-object relationship

The experience of subject and object is common to everyone. Like those who are awakened, be mindful of the real relationship between the two.

—Verse 106

To experience being a subject, a separate self, and also to experience the world as an object, something separate from us, is the common human perspective. This contemplation asks us to acknowledge this, but to also acknowledge our oneness with all of life, the truth that underlies our surface perception.

Notice the non-judgmental tone of this contemplation. Duality and non-duality are not pitted against each other. The common human experience of feeling separate from what we perceive is neither denied nor denigrated. We are simply asked to remember the awakened perspective of the underlying reality as well. We are one with all we perceive.

~

Practice feeling Oneness

- Think deeply about the idea that, underlying your everyday experience of being separate from what you see, exists another aspect of yourself that knows its oneness with everything.

- Notice that, if you become quiet, you can hold both perceptions at the same time.

- Stay here, marveling at how you can undulate between these two ways of seeing.

84.
The same Consciousness is in all bodies

Know that the Consciousness in your body is the same as the Consciousness in another's. Leaving aside all concern for your personal self, in time you will experience yourself pervading all of creation.

—Verse 107

Our physical bodies are the anchor for our sense of being a separate self. The practice below begins with the body but asks us to shift our attention from our personal concerns to the spark of Consciousness in ourselves and then to hold to the thought that this same spark—this same throbbing, luminous awareness—is also present in every other body.

Holding to this thought, we begin to experience ourselves as pervading all of creation—all beings, all things, all times, all places.

~

Practice thinking about your union with all

- Hold to the thought that the spark of Consciousness—the pulsing, luminous awareness—that is in your body is also present in everything else in the universe.

- Stay with this thought until you begin to experience yourself as pervading all beings, all things, all times, all places.

85.
No thoughts for support

Refrain from all thinking by freeing your mind of all supports.
Your individual self will merge with the great Self.

—Verse 108

We are constantly using thoughts, memories, stories, and beliefs to support our sense of being a separate self. In this meditation, we purposely disentangle ourselves from all of our ideas about ourselves and the world and then come to rest in the thought-free state of pure awareness.

Without thoughts to prop up our self-image, our individual sense of self releases its grip and merges into the experience of luminous pure awareness, the great Self of all.

Practice freeing your mind from thoughts

- Free your mind of all thoughts, memories, images, beliefs—anything that the mind regularly uses to orient itself.

- Rest in the thought-free space, and let your individual self merge into luminous, pure awareness, the great Self.

86.
Identify with Shiva and his attributes

Shiva is all knowing, all powerful, and all pervasive. Since you have these same divine qualities, you are similar to him. Recognize the Divine in yourself.

—Verse 109

Shiva is seen in this tradition as the highest Reality. The meditation is telling us that we are Shiva and that we, too, possess divine qualities. Even though these are huge ideas, by feeling our way into each quality, we find that they are actually present within us.

Identifying with the qualities of our highest nature counteracts our isolated sense of self. From the personal level, attributes like these—"all knowing, all powerful, and all pervasive"—can sound grandiose. But from the perspective of the Consciousness that lies at the core of our being, these qualities *are* our greater nature.

At some point in our evolution, we will need to make a choice as to which perspective we are going to live from. Once we have chosen to move beyond our individual self, such qualities become affirmations and can be particularly helpful in reinforcing our highest nature. By identifying with qualities like these, we can become them and can inhabit the state from which they arise.

Almost all mystical traditions have a version of this meditation, focusing on that particular tradition's favorite qualities of Self: love, kindness, awareness, presence, stillness…Once we grasp the principle behind this practice, it is possible to practice this meditation in our own, individual way.

~

Practice seeing yourself as the highest

- Repeat to yourself, "The highest principle is all knowing, all powerful, and all pervasive. I am this principle."

- Move from the ideas expressed by these words into the feelings they convey.

- Allow these transcendent qualities to awaken in you.

~

Practice seeing yourself as a divine quality

- Choose a quality of Self that you especially resonate with—timeless, boundless, loving, luminous, free…

- Repeat this quality to yourself or state that you are this quality—I am timeless, I am boundless, I am free…

- Gently move from the idea expressed by the word into the experience of it, until you become this quality.

87.
The universe arises as waves in me

Just as waves arise from water, flames from fire, and light rays from the sun, contemplate, "The different waves of Consciousness that emanate as the universe all arise in me."

—Verse 110

In the traditions of Self-recognition, there are two steps. The first is to recognize our most fundamental nature as pure conscious awareness. The second is to recognize our oneness with the entire manifest world that has arisen from the same Consciousness.

Building on the previous meditation, where we contemplated the divine qualities of our fundamental inner nature, here we externalize that awareness, recognizing that the magnificence of the entire universe is ours. The waves of Consciousness that flash forth as the appearance of the world all arise within us. The arising of waves from water, flames from fire, and rays of light from the sun symbolize the movement of the universal emanations of Consciousness—the movement of the formless into form. By contemplating these beautiful passages in nature, we awaken an ancient memory that we ourselves are all this.

~

Practice seeing yourself as the source of the universe

- Contemplate that just as waves arise from water, flames from fire, and light rays from the sun, the various waves of Consciousness that emanate as the universe arise in you.

88.
Whirl or dance—suddenly stop!

Whirl your body around and around and then, all at once, fall to the ground. When the swirling energy ends, you are in a wonderful state.

—Verse 111

Children have always known this one! The intensity of kinetic movement is wonderfully energizing. Giving ourselves over into the intensity of the energy, we shift out of thinking and into the experience of pure aliveness.

This meditation is a delightful example of how we can use anything that's physically enjoyable and energizing—whirling, dancing, sports, lovemaking—to shift ourselves into a higher state. The key here is to linger in the moment of stillness at the end of the activity and to savor the experience.

~

Practice doing and then stopping

- Throw yourself fully into anything physically enjoyable and vitalizing—whirling, dancing, lovemaking…
- When you stop, notice the feeling of pure aliveness. Stay here.

89.
The end of an intense mental impasse

When you experience a mental impasse, whether due to a lack of energy or to sheer ignorance, your mind will at some point dissolve from the intensity of the agitation. Become completely absorbed in the energy at the end of the agitation, and the awakened state will appear.

—Verse 112

As in the previous meditation, the focus here is on using intensity to catapult us into the thought-free state. In this meditation, we see that even the intensity of mental frustration can be a gateway to the non-dual state.

The intense frustration of a blocked situation will at some point cause our mind to give up. In this moment of mental collapse, we spontaneously shift into the thought-free state for a time. If we are aware of this mental shift and choose to stay in the pure energy of the experience, this energy itself, free of all thought, will carry us beyond our separate self into the experience of pure being. This is why people often report moments of tremendous insight that come when they finally stop struggling.

As with all of the meditations on life experiences, we can practice this meditation in two ways: we can recall a memory of such an experience, or we can catch the moment as it occurs in our life. Employing memory, which is what we do in the practice below, is one way to be prepared when such a moment arises spontaneously.

~

Practice experiencing a mental impasse

- Remember a time when you experienced a mental impasse, whether due to being exhausted or from just not knowing what to do.

- Go to the moment when your mind collapsed and gave up all thinking.

- Hold your attention to this moment when you have stopped all mental struggle and notice that you are in a thought-free state. The intense energy of the frustration is now released from being trapped in your struggle.

- Stay with the freed energy and let it take you into the state of Oneness.

90.
Fix the eyes without blinking

Listen carefully as I reveal the entirety of this mystical tradition. Fix your eyes without blinking. The state of liberation will be there immediately.

—Verse 113

This famous open-eyed meditation came to be known as *bhairavi mudra*. In it, our awareness focuses both inward and outward simultaneously. We look out at life from the core of our being.

In this *mudra* our gaze is simultaneously directed inward and outward. Our awareness is deeply and unshakably centered in our inner being and, at the same time, it is extended—literally "thrown"—outward in all directions, evenly spread all around.

With this dual focus, our thinking spontaneously stops, and the distinction between inner and outer dissolves. There is just one. We are one with our experience. Only pure being, pure awareness, pure bliss remain.

~

Practice focusing inwards and outwards simultaneously

- With eyes open, turn your attention toward your inner being.

- Remaining deeply and unshakably centered in yourself, simultaneously extend your awareness outward so that it is evenly spread all around you, encompassing everything.

- Your gaze is wide open externally and, simultaneously, it is deeply centered in your inner awareness. You are looking out from an unshakable inner place.

- The distinction of outer and inner dissolve. Only pure being, pure awareness, pure bliss, pure Oneness remain.

91.
The interior sound

Having closed the ears and the lower openings, meditate on the inner space of the unstruck sound and enter the Eternal.

—Verse 114

In deep meditation, we can tune into the earliest vibrations of Consciousness as its energy first begins to move from pure potential toward form.

Remember that the term "unstruck sound" refers to the fact that this is an inner vibration and not a sound produced by the striking together of two external objects. To assist us in entering the inner space in which we will hear this inner vibration, we are instructed to apply two physical gestures known as *bandhas* or "locks." The first of these is to plug each ear with a finger to make it easier to focus on the subtle inner sound. The second is to pull up the perineum at the base of the torso to help contain energy in the body.

Once these locks are in place, we put our attention on the inner space—often called the inner temple—and we listen to the subtle inner sound.

Listening for the inner sounds with a quiet mind takes us to the subtlest and most exquisite levels of energy in our consciousness. Some hear these inner sounds as a subtle version of outer sounds, like the symphony of crickets at night, or tiny cymbals ringing, or rushing water, or distant thunder, or the sound of *OM* reverberating in infinity. For some the inner sounds are a dimension of inner music unlike anything they have heard before. And for some, these sounds are like the hum of life itself. In whatever ways this subtle vibration presents itself to you, once you find it, stay with it. It will take you into deeper dimensions and eventually to the deepest bliss of your being.

For anyone who is unfamiliar with applying locks in meditation, attempting them with this meditation might be distracting. If you find that, then you can choose to apply the locks metaphorically and to mentally set your intention to keep all openings of your body sealed so that all energy flows toward the sacred inner space.

~

Practice listening to the inner sound

- Sitting quietly, plug each ear with a finger, pull up the muscles of your perineum at the base of your torso, and meditate on the unstruck sound in the inner space.

- This inner vibration may sound like crickets at night, or like tiny cymbals ringing, or rushing water, or distant thunder, or exquisite inner music unlike any you have heard before, or the sound of *OM* reverberating in infinity, or the hum of life itself.

- However this inner pulse of Consciousness sounds to you, once you find the sound, stay with it.

- Meditate on the inner sound and the space in which it appears, letting it take you into the highest bliss of your being.

92.
Staring into a deep well

Steadily look into a bottomless darkness, such as in a deep hole or a well. Your mind will become free of thoughts and immediately dissolve.

—Verse 115

This meditation returns to a moment of simple life experience. When standing at the top of a well or deep hole, it can be hypnotic as we stare down into the abyss. Our senses probe into the bottomless darkness. In that moment, there can be the thrill of entering the unknown. We are to fix our attention right there. With nothing to hold onto but a bottomless darkness, our mind lets go and dissolves into the great mystery.

This meditation is another example of how life itself is full of opportunities to touch into the great unseen.

~

Practice looking into darkness

- When you come across anything that has a profound darkness, such as a deep hole or a well, look down into it steadily.

- As you stare into the abyss, let your mind dissolve into the bottomless darkness and merge into oneness with the great mystery of life.

93.
Wherever the mind goes is Shiva

Wherever your mind goes, whether to the outer world or the inner, there is Shiva [the all-pervasive Consciousness]! Where else can the mind go!

—Verse 116

This is a powerful idea, well worth contemplating. No matter where our mind goes, whether to the outer world or to the inner world, there is nowhere it can go that is not Consciousness. Every object, every state, every place, every thought, every tree, every atom, every universe, every mood, every memory, every dream...All this Shiva—nothing but Consciousness. There is only one Consciousness in the universe.

Contemplating that there is no place our mind can go, outer or inner, that is not made of Consciousness, we begin to lose our sense of separation. We feel the oneness of life.

~

Practice contemplating that your mind touches only Consciousness

- Contemplate, "Wherever my mind goes—whether to the outer world or to the inner world of thoughts, images, feelings, dreams—there is the all-pervasive Consciousness! Where else can my mind go! There is only one Consciousness."

94.
Whatever is sensed is Consciousness

Contemplate that the consciousness that flows through your senses as well as the objects of your senses are nothing but Consciousness. You will dissolve in a state of divine fullness.

—Verse 117

This meditation on experiencing Consciousness begins by feeling the flow of consciousness through our senses. As we experience consciousness moving through us and out to the objects of life, we are to contemplate that whatever is contacted by our organs of sense—whatever is seen, smelled, touched, heard, or tasted by us—this, too, is nothing but Consciousness. In the practice below, we are contemplating that the one who sees, the act of seeing, and that which is seen are all one Consciousness. As we hold to this awareness, our customary separation of ourselves from the objects we experience begins to dissolve into Oneness.

We can easily adjust this practice to include any of the senses. For example, as we read this book, we might feel consciousness flowing down our arm and into our fingers and the book we are holding, which is also Consciousness appearing in the form of the book.

This same flowing sequence can be applied to hearing, tasting, smelling…The following is a practice using sight.

~

Practice with an object you see

- Look at an object. Become aware that in this act of looking, Consciousness is flowing through your eyes and out to the object.

- Once you become steady in this awareness, understand that the object you are seeing is also nothing but Consciousness appearing in that form.

- The Consciousness that flows through your eyes out to the object, as well the object itself are nothing but Consciousness.

- Pause, and allow yourself to make the extraordinary shift into Oneness.

95.
The beginning and end of intensity

At the beginning and end of sneezing; or when in terror, sorrow, or confusion; or while fleeing from a battlefield; or in intense curiosity; or at the beginning or end of hunger; notice that this state of intensity is like the awakened state.

—Verse 118

In unexpected moments of intensity, our mind often spontaneously stops for an instant. The intensity of the situation momentarily overwhelms the mind, and we are catapulted into the thought-free state. This meditation asks us to focus our awareness on these precise moments.

The intensity of these experiences is nothing but pure life energy surging through us. By shifting our attention from our thoughts about the situation to the immediacy of the energy, we can notice how the experience is very much like the awakened state in which there is a sense of intense aliveness and an awareness that can feel spacious and timeless.

Contemplating our experience of peak intensity helps us understand the experience of our awakened consciousness. It also prepares us to catch these moments when they occur spontaneously so that we can learn to stay with the extraordinary energy and awakened perceptions.

Another text in this tradition, when discussing this practice, gives the delightful example of the experience of being chased by a wild elephant!

~

Practice thinking of intensity

- Remember a moment of intensity—a birth, a death, some-one saying "I love you" for the first time, a car accident, a sneeze, or any other intense event.

- Feel the exact moment when the intensity overwhelmed your mind and left you, for an instant, in a highly alert, timeless, spacious awareness.

- Stay with the experience as long as you can, understanding that it is a powerful glimpse of the awakened state.

96.
Letting go of the object of memory

When a strong memory is stirred, such as when seeing your homeland after a long time away, let go of all thoughts and self-concerns. The all-pervading, powerful nature of Consciousness will appear.

—Verse 119

This is a meditation on the memory of a deep love. The previous meditations on intensity have all been about events very much in the present moment. Here, we are shown how we can also employ the intensity of a deep feeling from the past to help us shift states in the present.

Usually, when a strong memory comes up, we become lost in thoughts about what has happened and drift out of the present into the past. In this meditation, we are to catch the moment of deep feeling in this memory and to stay present with it, letting it take us deep into the vastness of our Self.

As with all meditations on intensity, we need to be alert to what is happening and then remember to pivot out of thinking and into fully feeling the heightened energy. This allows the energy itself to help us shift into the awakened perspective of our highest Self.

The following example is of using a memory of an intense love to help us contemplate this experience.

~

Practice letting go of a memory

- Remember a time when you were deeply stirred by something or someone you loved.

- Isolate the profound feeling. Let go of any thoughts about the event or about yourself and sink more deeply into the feeling and intensity of the emotion itself.

- Fully enter this feeling in the present moment, allowing it to carry you into the immense fullness of Consciousness.

97.
Withdraw gaze

Fix your eyes on a particular object, then slowly withdraw your gaze from the object as well as from any thoughts or impressions of it. You will become an abode of the great Emptiness.

—Verse 120

Here we have another way of entering *bhairavi mudra*, where our gaze is directed inward and outward at the same time.

We begin this meditation by looking steadily at an object. Then, while continuing to gaze at this object, we slowly withdraw our attention from it, letting go of any thoughts about it and bringing our attention back to our inner Self. Because we're still looking at the object, our awareness is now out (with the object) and, at the same time, in (with our Self). Our eyes are open with our attention evenly spread all around us while simultaneously resting in the unshakable inner space of pure awareness. Thoughts fall away, and we enter the great Emptiness that contains all things.

~

Practice withdrawing your attention from an object

- Begin by looking steadily at any object of your choice.

- Keep your eyes open, and slowly withdraw your attention from the object as well as from any inner commentary about it.

- You still see the object, but your attention returns to your inner Self, your observing awareness, and stays anchored here.

- Your field of vision remains open and soft.

- You keep seeing the object, but your awareness is completely rooted like a tree in your inner Self.

- All separating thoughts drop away. Inner and outer become one. You enter the great Emptiness that contains all things.

98.
An intuition of intense devotion or longing

The type of intuition that arises from intense devotion in someone who is completely detached from all personal concerns is the sublime energy of Consciousness itself. Meditate regularly on the energy of this intuitive knowing, and it will lead you to the Eternal.

—Verse 121

The focus in this meditation is on the power of our love of Consciousness, our love of God. The intensity of our devotion to the Eternal awakens in us a direct intuitive knowing. By regularly meditating on the powerful energy of divine intuitive knowing, we become one with this knowing and its source.

~

Practice meditating on your love for life

- Meditate on your love of life or God or Consciousness.
- Feel deeply the profound energy of your devotion.
- Sense how there is a wisdom in this energy of devotion, a direct intuitive knowing of higher truths.
- Stay with this divine knowing and merge into the Eternal.

99.
One object, all else is empty

Focus intently on one particular object and notice that all other objects in your field of vision become empty. Contemplating the emptiness of everything else in the periphery of your vision, even though one object remains, you will slip into a state of tranquility.

—Verse 122

The mind is accustomed to a rapid succession of contrasting perceptions and thoughts. By holding steady to one object or thought, all other thoughts begin to subside. The normally dispersed energy of our mind starts to gather into a single point of awareness. We become centered and present.

In this variation on this classical yogic practice, once our focus becomes established, we are to open up our awareness without losing its central focus and to notice how everything in our peripheral vision seems to become vacuous—empty of the vivid reality that the object of our focus has. Where the verse speaks of "contemplating the emptiness of everything else," it means becoming aware of this, sensing it, with no discursive thought.

At this point we are aware of two things simultaneously—our object of focus and its empty periphery. This simultaneous perception can be done only from a state of unconditioned awareness, our awakened Self. A person cannot hold both the experience of the object and of the peripheral emptiness without being completely centered and aware.

As we begin to recognize the inherent emptiness of the objective world, all that is left is luminous Consciousness. Both outer and inner dissolve. We slip into a state of tranquility.

~

Practice with one object

- Steadily look at an object.

- Notice that all the other objects in your field of vision start to become less substantial, as if they were emptied of their own vivid reality.

- Contemplate the emptiness of everything in the periphery of your vision—everything other than your object of focus.

- Relax and release into a state of tranquility.

100.
Beyond the conventional pure and impure

The purity described by people of little understanding is not understood as purity by those who know the Self. In the highest Reality, there is no purity and impurity. Be free of these thoughts, and attain happiness.

—Verse 123

Concepts of "pure" and "impure" are common to most spiritual traditions. Such notions can be helpful at many stages of our inner work. From the awakened perspective, however, these are unnecessary judgments that trap our mind at a dualistic and divisive level of perception. In this regard, these distinctions are conceptual baggage and need to be let go.

From the awakened perspective, all of life is perfect as it is. It is part of the whole. It is Consciousness appearing in this form. If we're going to experience this truth, then at some point we need to let go of all sorts of judgment; we need to cease judging and release into the deep happiness that then comes.

Notice that the instruction is to be free of the thoughts of "pure" and "impure" and not to be free of the ethical behavior appropriate to our time and culture—actions that spontaneously arise out of our Self's inherent sense of oneness with others.

~

Practice looking beyond purity and impurity

- Contemplate that from the highest Reality, there is no such thing as purity and impurity. At this level, it is all just Consciousness.

- Be free of these judgments, and experience the true happiness of seeing from the highest perspective, through the eyes of Oneness.

101.
Reality is apparent, even in common folk

The reality of Consciousness is everywhere, even in common folk! Contemplating "there is nothing other than this one reality," you will enter the great non-dual state.

—Verse 124

The spiritual ego is one of the subtlest and most difficult aspects for us to see in ourselves. This variation on seeing the oneness of all life emphasizes the conscious inclusion of those people and things that we judge to be inferior or different from ourselves. Even these— particularly these!—are to be included in our practice of seeing God everywhere and in everything and everyone. This meditation addresses any sense of spiritual superiority in which we may be inadvertently indulging. Any judgment or sense of difference toward others tightens our heart and impedes our full sense of oneness with all that is.

The same Consciousness is in those whom we feel are "ordinary" or not spiritually awake—perhaps street people, the lost, the seemingly unconscious, the ignorant, the poor, the deluded, or even just those of the other political party...To contemplate that the same Consciousness is all these people is a powerful way to keep the sense of separation from others from creeping into our hearts.

~

Practice looking at how you see people in your life

- Take a careful look at yourself. Make note of all the people in your life you may subtly judge as inferior or from whom you hold yourself apart.

- Take your time with this. Some of them may be obvious. Others can be very subtle—and may be masquerading in your mind as other forms of discrimination.

- Feel how any sense of superiority in you creates a sense of separation from others and causes your heart to contract.

- Once you have identified the people you hold yourself separate from, remind yourself that there is only one loving Consciousness everywhere. That which you hold so dear is as present in these people as it is in you.

- Hold the thought, "There is nothing other than this one reality," until your sense of separation dissolves in the sublime recognition of your oneness with everyone and everything.

102.
The same in honor and dishonor

See friend and foe as equal, honor and dishonor as the same. Knowing the Self to be complete and full, you will become perpetually happy.

—Verse 125

Being able to remain balanced in the face of emotional extremes helps to strengthen our connection to our center, from where we can look at life from the highest perspective. Ordinarily, our sense of personal self is buoyed by what is emotionally supportive and deflated by what opposes us. We become attached to one and averse to the other. We are pulled out of our center.

If we can remain anchored in the knowledge that the same one Consciousness appears as all our experiences, we begin to see how all the extremes are equal—all part of the fullness of Consciousness. When we remember this, the powerful grip of these emotional currents is diminished. We can then transcend our attachment and aversion to the polarities of friend and foe, honor and dishonor. Seeing the same Consciousness in everything and everyone, we become supremely happy.

Remember that such experiences can elicit extreme reactions in us. The very intensity of these emotions lends great power to this contemplation.

~

Practice seeing all as equal

- Remembering that Consciousness has become everything and everyone, contemplate seeing friend and foe, honor and dishonor as the same.

- Knowing that Consciousness is full and complete, you will be perpetually happy.

103.
Free of attachment and aversion to others

Dwell on neither aversion nor attachment toward anyone, and remain in the center. Free of both of these, divine awareness blossoms in your heart.

—Verse 126

This meditation and the preceding one both focus on attaining the divine state of equal vision. In the previous meditation, we attain this state by mentally affirming that the same Consciousness is present in all of life. Here, we approach the same state of divine evenness of vision through discipline—by consciously choosing to not indulge any thoughts of hatred or attachment toward anyone.

One approach is choosing what to do, and the other is choosing what not to do. The embracive nature of this text is showing that both means are effective and that they complement each other.

Both thoughts of aversion toward another and wishes to cling to another belong to our reactive, separate self. Indulging such thoughts only traps us further in our sense of disconnection from the inherent goodness of life and from the strength and the broad understanding of our own true Self. Thoughts of hating someone or of wanting to grasp onto to someone, which is different from loving them, can only bind us in weakness and limitation. Once we are freed of such thoughts, divine awareness blossoms.

~

Practice going beyond aversion and attachment

- Contemplate the binding, weakening, and delusive nature of thoughts of aversion and clinging.

- Once you are clear on how such thoughts pull you out of your true Self, set your intention not to dwell on such thoughts toward anyone.

- Remain in your center, free from both attachment and aversion, and feel divine awareness blossoming in your heart.

104.
That which cannot be grasped yet penetrates all

That which cannot be known, that which cannot be grasped, that which is void, that which penetrates even non-existence... all this should be contemplated as Consciousness! It will end in enlightenment.

—Verse 127

This meditation expands our mind far beyond its familiar boundaries. The mind's nature is such that it forms an internal sense of even ungraspable concepts such as these. These huge ideas, like everything else in creation, are made of Consciousness and are appearing to us in Consciousness. By asserting that even these seemingly unknowable aspects of our experience, too, are Consciousness, we are able to include them as part of the whole. As we contemplate this, we cease being alienated from our own thoughts and experience—even thoughts of the unknown. We spontaneously enter into the state of unity.

~

Practice looking at the nature of the unknowable

- That which cannot be known, that which cannot be grasped, that which is void, that which penetrates even non-existence—contemplate that all this too is nothing but Consciousness.

105.
Eternal space

Focus your attention on any external expanse of space and contemplate that the very nature of the space is eternal, without support, empty, all-pervasive, and free from limitation. With practice, you will enter the great state beyond space.

—Verse 128

In this meditation, while focusing on external space as we have in previous exercises, we are now adding to our contemplation a consideration of the qualities this space has in common with pure awareness—that it is eternal, independent, empty, all-pervasive, and boundless. Because these qualities of space are familiar to us, they provide a clear example of each of these more transcendent aspects of awareness. By meditating on these qualities, we can "feel" them—we can sense their inherent nature. Our mind expands, and we find ourselves in the sublime state beyond all thought.

~

Practice focusing on the nature of space

- Focus on—or recall a memory of—an expansive external space.

- Let your awareness open, extending out into the natural beauty. Feel how the very nature of the space is eternal, without support, empty, all-pervading, and free from limitation.

- Stay with the feeling of each of these qualities, allowing them to take you into the great state beyond all space and thought.

106.
Wherever the mind goes, remove it!

Wherever the mind goes, immediately withdraw it. Having nothing to lean on, your mind becomes free of agitation.

—Verse 129

This meditation is another, wonderful variation on how to enter the thought-free state.

The mind's natural state is a relaxed, spacious awareness. In this open awareness, thoughts, images, feelings all appear and disappear. Our attention can move from our spacious awareness into any of these dimensions of experience. This is natural. This is how we explore life. The problem comes when we forget to return to our Self. It is this returning to our true Self that lies at the core of all spiritual practice.

In this meditation, we become alert to the moment the mind fixates on anything and immediately withdraw it. Whether this is an external object or an internal feeling or thought is immaterial. Once we can feel this pattern of movement and then fixation— which is, in itself, an amazing thing to observe—we are to practice immediately withdrawing our mind from the object. For a moment, then, our mind returns to its source, open awareness. The untrained mind immediately goes out again to another object to lean on! It can be shocking to see how addicted our mind is to leaning on objects and how unfamiliar our mind is with returning to open awareness and resting there for a while.

Rather than trying to stop the mind, this practice focuses on our ability to move our attention and bring it back to open awareness at will by simply not letting the mind fixate on anything.

It can be helpful to approach this practice playfully. See how long you can go before becoming "parked" on something. You can start with five seconds so that you begin to develop some confidence!

Remember, you are not the movements of your mind. You are the awareness in which the movements occur. The focused mind is a wonderful tool you possess, and the mind will respond to clear, repeated directions. An old Chinese saying seems pertinent here: "You can't stop birds from lighting in a tree, but you can keep them from building a nest!"

This practice can be done both with eyes either open or closed. If you do it with your eyes open, keep your gaze gently moving or very soft.

~

Practice withdrawing focus

- Wherever the mind goes, immediately withdraw it from that thought or object.
- Do this over and over.
- Having nothing to lean on, your mind will gradually become free of all agitation and return to its original home, the open awareness of your true Self.
- Rest here.

107.
Repeat the name Bhairava

Bhairava—dispeller of fear, giver of all, the one who pervades the entire universe. Unceasingly, repeat the name Bhairava and become one with Consciousness.

—Verse 130

Bhairava is one of the many names in this tradition given to Consciousness, the state of Oneness. It is also one of the names of Shiva. In particular, this name represents the fearless aspect of the state of Oneness. When we repeat the name Bhairava while remaining aware of what this name represents—dispeller of fear, giver of all, the one who pervades the entire universe—our mind begins to resonate with these qualities. Our awareness shifts from our separate, individual identity to the sublime state of luminous being.

This meditation on repeating the name of Bhairava engages the inherent power of our love of the Infinite. Since names for Consciousness vary with each tradition, you may wish to substitute for this particular name whatever term best resonates in your heart—awareness, Consciousness, freedom, God, Mother, love, *Hamsa*…

The attributes—dispelling fear, giving of all, and pervading the universe—are universal and have their own effect when contemplated.

~

Practice repeating a divine name

- Repeat the name Bhairava—or any name of Consciousness that you love—while contemplating the qualities of dispelling fear, giving of all, and pervading the entire universe.

- Continue repeating the name while contemplating these qualities until your awareness begins to shift from your sense of separate individuality into the sublime state of pure luminous being.

108.
From the little "I" to the big "I"

While making assertions like, "I am," "This is mine," and so on, let your mind go to that pure sense of "I" that exists without any thoughts for support. Contemplating this pure sense of "I," become supremely peaceful.

—Verse 131

In all the different roles we play in life, there is one constant: our sense of being, our sense of "I." Usually, we identify with ideas about ourselves as well as with our roles in life: "I am a student," "I am a parent," "I am a yogi," "I am a businessperson," "I am a success," "I am a failure."

In this meditation, we focus on the pure "I" without going on to any other thoughts. This "I" is your sense of pure being, pure awareness—prior to any ideas or roles. Its very nature is simple, alive, free, and whole. Meditating on this "I," we become supremely peaceful.

~

Practice focusing on the pure "I"

- Focus on the pure sense of "I." This "I" is your sense of being, free of any association, pure awareness—prior to any thoughts and feelings.

- Meditate on this "I" and become supremely peaceful.

109.
Repeat the divine qualities

"Eternal, omnipresent, without dependence on any support, all-pervasive, Lord-of-all-that-is"—meditate every moment on the meaning of these words, and you will attain these qualities.

—Verse 132

In this meditation, we repeatedly contemplate the qualities of Consciousness, penetrating into their essence. "Eternal, omnipresent, without dependence on any support, all-pervasive, Lord-of-all-that-is"—by constantly thinking deeply about the profound meaning of these words, we begin to enter into the sublime experience that they point toward.

~

Practice focusing on the divine qualities

- "Eternal, omnipresent, without dependence on any support, all-pervasive, Lord-of-all-that-is"—hold each of these qualities in your mind until you get a clear sense of what it means.

- Stay with each quality until it begins to activate the ancient memory and experience of this dimension in your consciousness.

- Keep returning to these words and what they represent until these dimensions of consciousness become more and more familiar to you. In time, they will become a constant part of your experience.

- No longer disconnected from these sublime aspects of yourself, you will feel complete.

110.
The illusory nature of the world

Contemplate that the appearance of this world is like that of a magic show, devoid of any essential reality. For what is real in a magic show! By firmly thinking like this, you will experience great peace.

—Verse 133

A magic show involves something that is not what it seems. On the surface, one thing appears to be happening. In reality, something else is going on. What we think we are seeing has no reality to it. How amazing!

Here is yet another meditation using a delightful life experience to help us shift into divine perception.

When we contemplate that the whole universe is like a magic show—a momentary and superficial appearance in Consciousness, with no substantive reality to it—then our mind's constructed drama of life can fall away. We can glimpse past the veil of thought and see into the timeless presence that dances behind all appearance.

Perceiving for ourselves the magical nature of time and space, we are filled with delight. There is no more reason to struggle; we are filled with great peace.

~

Practice seeing the world as magic

- With eyes open or closed, contemplate that the appearance of this entire world is like that of a magic show, devoid of any essential reality. For what is real in a magic show!

- Repeatedly thinking like this, let go into the deep peace that comes with this understanding.

111.
Changeless Self: empty world

In the timeless, changeless Self, how can there be any knowledge or activity? External objects are dependent on our knowledge of them. Without this limited knowledge, the universe is void [of all differentiation].

—Verse 134

The Self is not bound by time, space, or form. Only the individual self experiences the objective world as separate from itself.

This meditation encourages us to think deeply about the nature of the Self and the nature of our thoughts and perception. It is our limited knowledge of the world that traps our attention in surface differences and blocks our ability to experience our timeless Self and the Oneness that is the foundation of all life. Here, we are asked to think deeply about all of this. If we do, we will begin to see the entire universe as it truly is—devoid of all surface differences and nothing but Consciousness.

~

Practice contemplating the illusory nature of the world

- Enter into the timeless presence of your greater Self.

- Contemplate the illusory nature of the surface appearance of life.

- Let all knowledge of differences dissolve.

- Without any thoughts about differences, the entire world is your very own Self.

112.
Neither bondage nor liberation

There is neither bondage nor liberation for me. These ideas only intimidate the fearful. Just as the sun is reflected in water, this entire universe is like a reflection in the mind.

—Verse 135

The notions of "bondage" and "liberation" can be quite helpful at certain stages of our spiritual growth. When we feel trapped in a sense of separation, the very idea of liberation can give us hope.

However, even the most sublime concepts can keep us entangled in the endless loops of our mind. By going beyond our most prized spiritual beliefs—in this instance, "bondage" and "liberation"—we step out of our own judgments and projections. Without thoughts filtering our perception, the dream-like quality of life becomes apparent. Like sunlight reflecting on water, the entire universe is only a reflection appearing in our mind. Once Consciousness becomes free of even the highest ideas, it appears in its own primordial beauty.

~

Practice seeing the world as your own reflection

- Let go of even high spiritual thoughts such as "bondage" and "liberation."

- Contemplate that, just as the sun is reflected in the surface of water, the entire world is nothing but a reflection in your mind.

113.
Withdrawing the senses from pain and pleasure

All contact with pain and pleasure comes through the senses. Withdraw your attention from your senses. Stay firm in your Self, and abide in your own true nature.

—Verse 136

After many high philosophical meditations and just before its ending, the text returns here to a foundational yogic practice. In this way, the *Vijnana Bhairava* once more brings the highest abstractions back, lovingly, to the body and to our daily life. Philosophy, play, beauty, magic, discipline—all are honored, all are seen as divine aspects of the One.

This meditation is another variation on the practice of *pratyahara* where we intentionally withdraw our attention from our senses and bring it back into our Self.

How admirable is the person who can hold steady in the face of pain and pleasure. The experience of pain and pleasure can keep us trapped on the surface of our experience, missing life's underlying beauty and mystery. Most of us can intuitively understand how pain is a trap, but the fact is that even pleasure can pull us out of our center. It is deeply empowering to know that in the face of distracting pain and pleasure, we can withdraw our attention from our senses and hold steady in our true Self.

~

Practice withdrawing from pain and pleasure

- Contemplate what it would be like to withdraw your attention from your senses when faced with pain or pleasure.

- Repeat this practice enough times so that in the future, if needed, you have a clear sense of how to do it.

- Feel how empowering it is to know that you have this capacity to pull back from pain or pleasure and into your true Self.

114.
The knower and the known
are the same

All things are revealed by knowledge of the Self, and the Self is revealed by all things. Their nature being the same, one should contemplate that the knower and the known are one and the same.

—Verse 137

This teaching that the knower and the known—the subject and the object, the experiencer and the experienced, the Self and the universe—are one is perhaps the most famous and beloved of all the non-dual teachings.

This final meditation begins with the subtle observation that the knower and the known both reveal, meaning that they illuminate each other. The knower, the observing Self, shines awareness onto the known, the object of perception. The very fact that there is a known shows that there is a knower! In this way, both knower and known have the same basic nature, to illuminate.

Since they both have the same nature, we should understand that knower and known are one.

Being, illumination, and Oneness all come together in this final meditation.

~

Practice thinking about the knower and known

- Contemplate that the knower (you) and the known (the universe) are one.

- Contemplate, "I and my experience are one."

Acknowledgements

It is to the scholar Jaideva Singh that I owe perhaps the greatest debt. It was his translation into English of the *Vijnana Bhairava* and his inspired commentary that first opened me to the extraordinary world of these meditations.

I also want to thank the unknown author of this text who passed on these practices in such a way that we can still benefit from their timeless truth.

And it was through the company of Swami Muktananda that I, and so many others, came to know of these teachings and to understand the nature of the Self. It is hard to find words to express the gratitude I feel.

Swami Lakshman Joo, Paul Reps, Swami Satyasangananda, and Daniel Odier were also greatly helpful through their translations and their published insights into the *Vijnana Bhairava*.

This book would not exist in this form without the help of many other people.

I wish to thank Nancy Fischer for her help with the translation as well as every aspect of the book from its very inception. Carmen Mascarenas for selfless hours of transcription and for keeping me organized—a rather large undertaking. Deborah Dungan for her invaluable help in editing the many drafts of the manuscript. Cynthia Franklin, whose clarity and insights into the meditations were inspiring. Robert Wempner for many years of supporting this work. David Cunningham and Janet Clow for their years of encouragement and also help with editing. Michael Omkar Connolly, Karen Shatar, Maria Gale, Angelique Cook-Lowry, Jim Carson for their sage input and help with the commentaries. And Susan Henoch for her laser-focused support in moving this to publication.

Everyone's company, present and past, made this a joy to do.

About the Author

Lee Lyon has taught meditation to more than ten thousand people worldwide. In the last forty years, he has developed an approach he calls Integrative Meditation, which is designed to bring together the many varied and extraordinary aspects of each person's consciousness with their sense of their own innermost being. Lyon has developed many meditation courses and has trained more than three hundred meditation teachers.

In 1999, Lyon established the Foundation for Integrative Meditation in Santa Fe, New Mexico, where he is based. He now works with people individually as well as in year-long training courses.

Lightning Source UK Ltd.
Milton Keynes UK
UKHW011424030720
365982UK00002B/159